1st EDITION

Perspectives on Diseases and Disorders

Breast Cancer

Carrie Fredericks
Book Editor

PERSPECTIVES
On Diseases & Disorders

GALE
CENGAGE Learning

Detroit • New York • San Francisco • New Haven, Conn • Waterville, Maine • London

Christine Nasso, *Publisher*
Elizabeth Des Chenes, *Managing Editor*

For more information, contact:
Greenhaven Press
27500 Drake Rd.
Farmington Hills, MI 48331-3535
Or you can visit our Internet site at gale.cengage.com

LIBRARY OF CONGRESS CATALOGING-IN-PUBLICATION DATA

Breast cancer / Carrie Fredericks, book editor.
    p. cm. — (Perspectives on diseases and disorders)
   Includes bibliographical references and index.
    ISBN 978-0-7377-4244-2 (hardcover)
   1. Breast—Cancer—Popular works. I. Fredericks, Carrie.
   RC280.B8 B6655622
   616.99'449—dc22

                                        2008026070

Printed in the United States of America
1 2 3 4 5 6 7 12 11 10 09 08

CONTENTS

INTRODUCTION

For more than 180,000 women every year, the words, "You have breast cancer" are life-altering. Breast cancer has been known for thousands of years. First discussed almost five thousand years ago in ancient Egypt, a breast cancer–like condition was described in early writings. Throughout the centuries breast cancer and its diagnosis and treatment have been described and illustrated by many physicians and scientists. The knowledge of breast cancer causes has changed dramatically, especially in the last thirty years. Researchers now know that breast cancer is not just a single disease. There are many different types of breast cancer, and each can affect a woman in different ways. But many strides are being made in the areas of breast cancer detection and treatment research.

For many women the possibility that cancer may exist in their breasts is something hard to face. Breast cancer survivor and author Domini Stuart states, "It's a strange thing, searching carefully for something you really don't want to find. When you're actually afraid of what you might find, there's a powerful temptation not to look at all."[1] But not looking at all does not affect whether cancer is present. That is where breast cancer detection comes in. There are two different types of testing for breast cancer. Screening tests are done when a patient has no known symptoms of the disease. Diagnostic tests are done when cancer is suspected or already known to exist.

Several new types of detection methods are being used more and more often in the case of breast cancer. One of these is digital mammography. In this test, traditional X-ray film is replaced with sensors that convert the

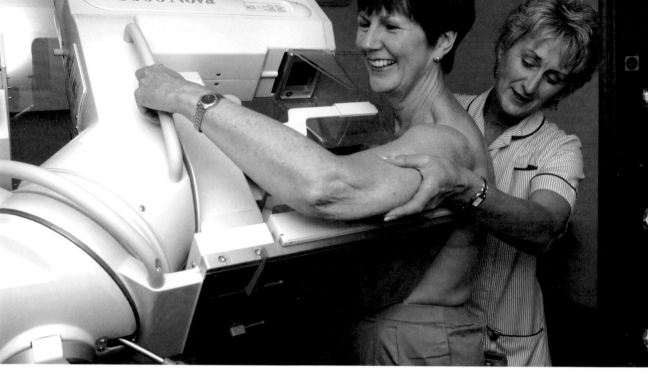

The war against breast cancer has been aided by several new detection methods like digital mammography. (Ian Miles-Flashpoint Pictures/Alamy)

X-rays into signals that are able to be seen on computer screens instead of having to be developed like traditional X-ray films. The process is very much the same as a traditional mammogram and yields the same type of mammography pictures. These pictures still have to be seen by a radiologist (a doctor who specializes in X-rays) to detect the presence of cancer.

One of the major advantages to digital mammography is that it is sometimes able to detect unusual lesions that may not be picked up by X-ray mammography. This is often the case in women with dense breast tissue. Dense breast tissue contains different types of tissue than a less dense breast, and scientists are beginning to find that this can lead to an increased breast cancer risk. In some cases the risk can be five times higher than women with less dense tissue.

Another type of detection in use is ultrasound. This procedure uses sound waves aimed through the tissue to create a picture of the inside of the breast. Ultrasound is able to more accurately evaluate known lesions when used in connection with mammography.

One area of detection that is very personal for some women is genetic testing. For the small percentage of women who carry the breast cancer gene mutations, the risk of eventually having breast cancer or ovarian cancer is at least seven times higher. According to the National Cancer Institute, 85 percent of women who test positive for these genetic variations will get breast cancer sometime in their lifetime. For some women the choice of finding out whether they are carrying abnormal variations of the breast cancer gene can be agonizing. Do they wait and see what happens? Do they have the test and then have to make pre–cancer-treatment decisions without knowing if or when the cancer will ever appear? Do they give up having children by removing their ovaries, which reduces their cancer risk? In a *New York Times* article by reporter Amy Harmon, Deborah Linder discusses her difficult choices after genetic testing showed she had a very high chance of developing breast cancer: "It could be growing inside of me right now. We could find it at any time."[2] Linder eventually decided to have a preventative double mastectomy. Because of the extensive personal and family issues that are part of this kind of cancer detection, genetic counseling is always recommended before undergoing any genetic testing.

Experimental detection methods are used also in early research stages. One of these, the PET (positron emission tomography) scan shows great potential in assessing cancer in lymph nodes and whether cancer still exists after chemotherapy and/or radiation. In a PET scan the patient is injected with a small dose of radioactive material, which is taken up by active cells. These active cells often indicate rapid cancer growth, and their presence assists the radiologist in determining the extent of the cancer.

In Britain, the University of Bolton's Centre for Research and Innovation is developing a bra that will detect the early stages of breast cancer. In a *BBC News* article, research director Elias Siores describes the science behind this development: "The cancer detection is based on the principle that metabolic activity and vascular circulation in both pre-cancerous tissue and the area surrounding a developing breast cancer is almost always higher than in normal breast tissue. This process results in an increase in regional internal and external temperatures on the breast."[3] Using microwave technology, the bra is designed to detect irregular temperature changes in a woman's breasts.

Another promising detection test in development is the saliva test. Charles Streckfus, a professor of diagnostic sciences at the University of Texas Dental Branch at Houston, explains that breast cancer causes changes in the proteins that are found in an individual's saliva. Scientists have now identified forty-nine saliva proteins that would help distinguish between healthy women and women with breast tumors. This testing method could begin the U.S. governmental approval process within the next several years.

For women with breast cancer, life is never the same. Appearance-altering surgery, harsh treatments, and agonizing decisions are all part of the process and are often overwhelming. But for many women, breast cancer detection methods are a way to have some control over a very frightening aspect of their health.

Notes

1. Domini Stuart, "Breast Cancer Survivor—Early Detection: Domini's Story," *Breasthealth*, September 2004. www.breasthealth.com.
2. Quoted in Amy Harmon, "Cancer Free at 33, but Weighing a Mastectomy," *New York Times*, September 16, 2007. www.nytimes.com.
3. Quoted in BBC News, "Smart Bra to Detect Early Cancer," September 27, 2007. http://news.bbc.co.uk.

CHAPTER 1

Understanding Breast Cancer

An Overview of Breast Cancer

Richard M. McCartney, Teresa G. Odle, and Tish Davidson

In the following selection Richard M. McCartney, Teresa G. Odle, and Tish Davidson provide an overview of breast cancer covering characteristics, causes, diagnosis, treatments, and prognosis. Although there are several main risk factors for breast cancer, it can strike anyone, regardless of how many risk factors an individual has. There are myriad treatment options, and treatments are usually individualized for every breast cancer case. As more advances are made in breast cancer research, prognosis for this disease continues to improve.

McCartney is a fellow of the American College of Surgeons. Odle and Davidson are science and medical writers.

Photo on previous page. Education and early detection are the keys to controlling breast cancer. (Bob Pardue/Alamy)

B reast cancer is caused by the development of malignant (cancerous) cells in the breast. Cancer cells are characterized by uncontrolled proliferation (growth) that results in tumor formation. If untreated,

SOURCE: Richard M. McCartney, Teresa G. Odle, and Tish Davidson, "Breast Cancer," *The Gale Encyclopedia of Medicine*, 2007. Reproduced by permission of Gale, a part of Cengage Learning.

malignant cells will invade normal tissue locally and spread throughout the body in a process called metastasis.

A woman's breast is made up of clumps of cells (glands) that, when stimulated by the proper hormones, secrete milk into a network of small tubes (ducts) that collect the milk and carry it to the nipple. The breast also contains fatty tissue, lymph vessels, and blood vessels. Breast cancer most often begins in the cells that line the ducts (ductal cancer.) Groups of glands in breast tissue are called lobules. Cancer can also begin in the lobules (lobular cancer) and much more rarely in other tissues of the breast.

Characteristics of Breast Cancer

Depending on where in the breast the cancer starts, it develops certain characteristics that are used to classify breast cancer into subtypes. Ductal carcinoma begins in the ducts. Lobular carcinoma has a pattern involving the lobules or glands. The more important classification of breast cancer is related to the tumor's capability to invade and spread, as this characteristic defines the disease as a true cancer. The stage before invasive cancer is called in situ, meaning that the early malignancy is located in one spot and has not yet spread. For example, ductal carcinoma in situ is considered a minimal breast cancer.

The primary tumor begins in the breast itself, but once it becomes invasive, it may move beyond the breast to the regional lymph nodes. Cells from the tumor also break off and travel through the lymphatic system and blood vessels to other parts of body where they form new tumors. This process is called metastasizing.

The lymphatic system carries lymph throughout the body. Lymph is a clear fluid that contains immune system cells that fight infection. It moves through a system of lymph channels and lymph nodes. In the nodes, lymph is filtrated and foreign material and dead cells are removed. Eventually lymph drains back into the bloodstream.

Nearly all organs in the body have a primary lymph node group filtering fluid that comes from that organ. In the breast, the primary lymph nodes are under the armpit, or axilla. Classically, a primary tumor that begins in the breast first spreads to the regional lymph nodes. Cancer cells may also invade blood vessels at their site of origin. When cancer cells enter the blood vessels, the circulatory system provides a way for the cancer to spread to other distant parts of the body.

Breast cancer tends to follow this classic progression, although it often becomes systemic or widespread early in the course of the disease. By the time one can feel a lump in the breast, it is often 0.4 in (1 cm) in diameter and contains roughly a million cells. Estimates suggest it may take 1–5 years for a tumor this size to develop. Dur-

Stages of Breast Cancer

Stage	Size and Location of Cancer
Stage 1	• No larger than 2 cm • No cancer in lymph nodes
Stage 2	• Between 2 and 5 cm • Cancer is in lymph nodes
Stage 3A	• Larger than 2 cm or smaller than 5 cm but is in lymph nodes, which have grown into each other
Stage 3B	• Cancer is in tissues near the breast or is in lymph nodes inside the chest wall
Stage 4	• Cancer has spread beyond the armpit or to other organs

Taken from: Richard M. McCartney, Teresa G. Odle, and Tish Davidson, "Breast Cancer," *The Gale Encyclopedia of Medicine*, Jacqueline L. Longe, ed. Detroit: Thomson Gale, 2007.

ing that time, the cancer cells may be spreading to other parts of the body.

When primary breast cancer spreads, it first usually spreads to the axillary lymph nodes in the armpit. This type of spread is called regional metastasis. If the cancer spreads elsewhere, either by lymphatic or blood-borne spread, the condition is called systemic metastasis. Systemic metastasis can involve several different organ systems in the body. Favorite sites of systemic involvement for breast cancer are the lung, bones, liver, and the skin and soft tissue. The number of regional lymph nodes containing cancer cells remains the single best indicator of whether or not the cancer has become widely metastasized. Because tests to discover metastasis in other organs may not be sensitive enough to reveal minute tumors, the evaluation of the axillary nodes for regional metastasis becomes important in making treatment decisions for this disease.

> **FAST FACT**
>
> Roughly two hundred thousand women develop breast cancer each year.

If breast cancer spreads to other major organs of the body, its presence will compromise the function of those organs. Death is the result of extreme compromise of vital organ function.

Who Is Affected?

Every woman is at risk for breast cancer. If she lives to be 85, there is a one out of eight (13%) chance that she will develop breast cancer at some time during her life. As a woman ages, her risk of developing breast cancer rises dramatically regardless of her family history. The breast cancer risk of a 25-year-old woman is only one out of 19,600; by age 45, it is one in 93. In fact, fewer than 5% of cases are discovered before age 35, and the majority of all breast cancers are found in woman over age 50.

In 2007, about 178,000 new cases of breast cancer were diagnosed. About 40,000 women die of breast cancer each year. Deaths from breast cancer are declining in recent years, a reflection of earlier diagnosis from screening mammograms and improving therapies.

Causes and Symptoms

Breast cancer does not have a single cause. Genetic, environmental, and lifestyle factors all play a role in determining who gets breast cancer. Although men can get breast cancer, women are 100 times more likely to develop the disease.

There is some debate about the importance of various risk factors for developing breast cancer. Some of these risk factors that increase the likelihood of getting breast cancer include:

- age. Eighty percent of breast cancers are found in women over age 50.
- a family history of breast cancer in a mother or sister. This is thought to double the risk of developing the disease.
- carrying the BRCA1 and BRCA2 genes. Women with these genes account for 5–10% of breast cancer cases and have an 80% chance of developing breast cancer at some time during their life.
- having first menstruation before age 12 or entering menopause after age 55.
- having no children or having a first child after age 30.
- daily alcohol consumption of two drinks or more.
- obesity and a high fat diet.
- breast exposure to radiation (e.g., in treatment of other cancers).
- postmenopausal hormone replacement therapy (HRT) with a combination estrogen/progesterone drug. Estrogen alone does not appear to increase risk. The longer a woman used HRT, the more her risk appeared to increased.

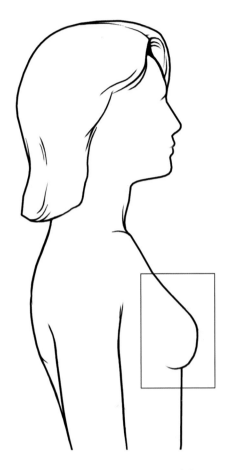

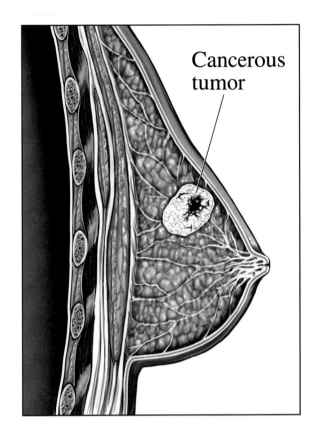

Cancerous
tumor

In this diagram a
cancerous tumor is
shown growing within a
female breast. (**Nucleus
Medical Art, Inc./Alamy**)

• history of abnormal breast biopsies or previous history of breast cancer.

Although these are recognized risk factors, some women with multiple risk factors never get breast cancer, while . . . women with no known risk factors do. Having several risk factors may boost a woman's chances of developing breast cancer, but the interplay of predisposing factors is complex.

Breast cancer cannot be prevented. Nevertheless, breastfeeding for more than one year, moderate exercise, such as walking 10 hours a week, and a diet low in saturated fats and high in fruits, vegetables, and whole grains have been shown in multiple studies to lower risk of developing breast cancer.

Not all lumps detected in the breast are cancerous. Fibrocystic changes in the breast are extremely common.

Also known as fibrocystic condition of the breast, fibrocystic changes are a leading cause of non-cancerous lumps in the breast. Fibrocystic changes can also cause pain, swelling, and discharge from the nipple. Non-cancerous (benign) lumps can be either solid or filled with fluid. Signs and symptoms of fibrocystic changes overlap with those of breast cancer. Complete diagnostic evaluation of any significant breast abnormality is essential to differentiate between fibrocystic changes and breast cancer. . . . Certain benign changes in the breast may now be linked to increased risk for breast cancer.

Self-Exams and Mammograms

All women are encouraged to do regular, monthly breast self-examinations. This involves feeling the breasts for any abnormal lumps or pain. A physician will also examine a woman's breasts during routine physicals and usually during regular gynecological examinations.

Initial screening for breast cancer is done with a mammogram. A mammogram is a low-dose, 2-view, x-ray examination of the breast. Mammography is non-invasive and causes no lasting pain (although the individual may feel temporary pain when the breasts are compressed for the mammogram.) The American Cancer Society recommends yearly mammograms for all women over age 40. Women at high risk for breast cancer may begin having mammograms at an earlier age. This test is usually covered by insurance. Mammography is helpful in detecting breast cancer too small to be identified on physical examination. However, 10–13% of breast cancer is not detected with mammography.

Because of the greater awareness of breast cancer in recent years, screening evaluations by examinations and mammography are performed much more frequently than in the past. The result is that the number of breast cancers diagnosed has increased, but the disease is being diagnosed at an earlier stage than previously. The earlier the stage of disease at the time it is discovered, the better the long-term outcome (prognosis) becomes.

If the mammogram suggests a breast abnormality, additional imaging tests may be done, including a repeat mammogram, magnetic resonance imaging (MRI) of the breast, or a breast ultrasound. None of these are invasive. A breast ultrasound can help distinguish between a fluid-filled cyst and a solid mass. If imaging confirms a solid lump is present, a biopsy may be done to definitively diagnose cancer.

Biopsy

Depending on the situation, different types of biopsy may be performed. The types include incisional and excisional biopsies. In an incisional biopsy, the physician takes a sample of tissue, and in excisional biopsy, the entire mass is removed. Fine needle aspiration biopsy and core needle biopsy are incisional biopsies.

Fine needle aspiration biopsy. In a fine needle aspiration biopsy, a fine-gauge needle is inserted into the abnormal area of the breast, and cells from the area suctioned into the needle. They are then quickly prepared for microscopic evaluation (cytology). A woman experiencing nipple discharge also may have a sample of the discharge taken for cytological evaluation. Fine needle aspiration is a simple procedure that can be done under local anesthesia, and the sample of cells will yield diagnostic information. . . .

Core needle biopsy. Core needle biopsies also are obtained under local anesthesia. The larger piece of tissue obtained with its preserved architecture may be helpful in confirming the diagnosis short of open surgical removal.

Excisional biopsy. Under some circumstances complete removal of the lump (lumpectomy) may be required. When performed, the excisional complete removal biopsy is a minimal outpatient procedure often done under local anesthesia.

Non-palpable lesions. As screening increases, small, non-palpable (unfelt) lesions discovered through mammography are becoming more common. In cases where the abnormality cannot be felt, the use of x-rays and computers to guide the needle for biopsy or to place markers for the surgeon performing the excisional biopsy are commonly employed. Some benign lesions can be fully removed by multiple directed core biopsies. These techniques are very appealing because they are minimally invasive; however, the physician needs to be careful to obtain a good sample.

Staging of Breast Cancer

Treatment of breast cancer depends on if, how far, and to what other organs the cancer has spread. This process of determining these factors is called staging.

Once diagnosis is established and before treatment begins, more tests are done to determine if the cancer has spread beyond the breast. These tests are likely to include a chest x-ray, blood tests, and liver function tests. Along with the liver function measured by the blood sample, the level of alkaline phosphatase, an enzyme from bone is also determined. A radionuclear bone scan may be ordered. This test looks at the places in the body to which breast cancer usually metastasizes. A CT [computerized tomography] scan also may be ordered. The physician will do a careful examination of the lymph nodes under the armpit (axillary lymph nodes) to assess likelihood of regional metastasis. Sometimes, the physician will remove all the axillary lymph nodes to assess breast cancer stage. However, studies show great success with sentinel lymph node biopsy. This technique removes the sentinel lymph node, or that lymph node that receives fluid drainage first from the area where the cancer is located. If this node is free of cancer, then it is likely that other axillary lymph nodes are also cancer free. This method saves women the discomfort and side effects associated with removing multiple lymph nodes in her armpit.

Using the results of these studies, the stage of cancer is defined for the patient. This helps establish a treatment protocol and prognosis. . . .

Treatment of Breast Cancer

Surgery, radiation, and chemotherapy are all used in the treatment of breast cancer. Depending on the cancer stage, they will be used in different combinations or sequences to effect an appropriate treatment strategy.

Surgery: Historically, surgical removal of the entire breast and axillary lymph nodes, along with the muscles down to the chest wall, was performed as the preferred therapy, (radical mastectomy). In the last 30 years, as it has been understood that breast cancer often spreads early, surgery remains a primary option, but other therapies have risen in importance. Recent studies have suggested that breast conserving treatment (as opposed to radical

Breast Surgery Options

Lumpectomy	Cancer and a small amount of normal tissue around it are removed. May remove lymph nodes in underarms.
Total mastectomy	The entire breast is removed.
Modified radical mastectomy	The entire breast is removed along with the lining above the chest muscles and some underarm lymph nodes.
Radical mastectomy	The entire breast is removed along with all underarm lymph nodes and all chest wall muscles.

Taken from: Breastcancer.org, 2008.

mastectomy) improves the quality of life for women. For patients who are diagnosed with advanced local disease, surgery may be preceded with chemotherapy and radiation therapy. The disease may locally regress, allowing traditional surgical treatment to those who could not receive it otherwise.

If tumor is less than 1.5 [inches] (4 cm) in size and located so that it can be removed without destroying the reasonable cosmetic appearance of the residual breast, just the primary tumor and a rim of normal tissue will be removed. The axillary nodes will still be removed for staging purposes, usually though a separate incision. This type of primary therapy is known as lumpectomy, (or segmental mastectomy), and axillary dissection. Because of the risk of recurrence in the remaining breast tissue, additional therapies (radiation, chemotherapy, etc.) are used to lessen the chance of local recurrence.

Sentinel lymph node biopsy, a technique for identifying whether cancer has spread to the lymphatic system, provides selective lymph node sampling and lessens the degree of surgical trauma the patient experiences. . . .

Supplemental Treatments

The definitive pathologic stage as determined after surgical treatment absolutely defines the extent of the surgery and adjuvant (supplemental) treatment required. Adjuvant therapies are treatments that occur after the primary treatment to help ensure that no microscopic disease exists and to help prolong patients' survival time.

Radiation therapy. Like surgical therapy, radiation therapy is a local modality—it treats only tissue exposed to radiation and not the rest of the body. Radiation is usually given post-operatively after surgical wounds have healed. After surgery, the pathologic stage of the primary tumor is known, and this aids in treatment planning. The extent of the local surgery also influences the planning. Radiation may not be needed at all after modified radical mastectomy for stage I disease, but is almost always needed when breast-preserving surgery is performed. The field of tissue exposed will vary based on the size of the tumor and the involvement of multiple nodes. Radiation is used as an adjunct to surgical therapy and is considered important in gaining local control of the tumor. In the past, radiation was sometimes used as an alternative to surgery. However, now that breast-preserving surgical protocols have been developed, primary radiation treatment of the tumor is no longer performed. Radiation also has an important role in the treatment of the patient with disseminated (widespread) disease, particularly if it involves the skeleton. Radiation therapy can affect pain control and help prevent bone fracture in this circumstance.

Chemotherapy. Survival after surgical treatment of breast cancer is improved by the addition of chemotherapy after surgery. Post-surgical chemotherapy in patients who have no evidence of residual disease is now performed on the basis that some patients have metastases that are not currently demonstrable. This occurs because it is unlikely that the surgeon has removed every single cancerous cell. Loose cancer cells may travel through the circulatory system and form new tumors elsewhere. Chemotherapy may also be given in some circumstances before surgery. . . . Adjuvant hormonal therapy or biotherapeutics may be added to the adjuvant chemotherapy as these treatments work through different routes.

Chemotherapy can be very effective but also debilitating. Individuals often have side effects that range from uncomfortable to serious. Symptoms of chemotherapy side effects are treated with both conventional drugs and complementary therapies.

Hormonal therapy. Many breast cancers, particularly those originating in postmenopausal women, are responsive to hormones. These cancers have receptors on their cells for estrogen. Part of the post-surgery primary tumor assessment is evaluation for the presence of these estrogen and progesterone receptors. If they are present on the cancer cells, altering the hormone status of the patient will inhibit tumor growth and have a positive impact on survival. Hormonal status may be changed with drug therapy. The drug tamoxifen binds to estrogen receptors on the cancer cells, so that the hormones cannot interact with the cells and stimulate their growth. If the patient has these receptors present, tamoxifen is commonly prescribed for five years as an adjunct to primary treatment. In women whose cancer cells have estrogen receptors, tamoxifen reduces the chance of breast cancer reoccurring by about 50%. . . .

In addition, a new group of drugs called aromatase inhibitors that block the enzymes that produce estrogen in postmenopausal (but not premenopausal) women have been used to treat both early and advanced breast cancer. . . .

Biotherapeutics. Biotherapeutics are a type of targeted therapy. Large amounts of antibodies of a single type (called monoclonal antibodies) that react with specific receptors on cancer cells are made in the laboratory. When given to the patient, they inactivate or destroy those cells containing that specific receptor, but do not react with other cells. Trastuzumab (Herceptin) and Lapatinib (Tykerb) target cells that contain a growth protein known as HER/2. Between 15% and 25% of women have breast cancer that responds to these drugs. Bevacizumab (Avastin) is a biotherapeutic used to treat breast cancer that has metastasized. It helps prevent tumors from becoming established by interfering with the growth of blood vessels into the tumor. Without access to nutrients in the blood, the tumors cannot increase in size. Biotherapeutics are normally used in addition to chemotherapy drugs.

Prognosis

The prognosis for breast cancer depends on the type and stage of cancer. Lymph node involvement is one of the best indicators of survival rates. The ten-year surviv-al rate for women with no lymph node involvement is 65–80%. If 1–3 nodes are involved, the ten-year survival rate is 35–65%. If more than four nodes contain cancer, the ten-year survival rate is 13–24%. Other factors such as tumor size and whether the cancer is sensitive to bio-therapeutics also affect survival rates.

Since most of the women who develop breast cancer have no risk factors, there is no good way to prevent the disease. Very high-risk women with a family history of breast cancer who carry the BRCA1 and BRCA2 genes may want to discuss preventative mastectomy with their physician. As of 2007, preventive surgery remained con-troversial.

Treatment Options for Breast Cancer

National Cancer Institute

In the following selection the National Cancer Institute discusses the many treatment options available to breast cancer patients. There are four main types of treatment: surgery, radiation, chemotherapy, and hormone therapy. According to the National Cancer Institute, treatment options are usually individualized, depending on the type and stage of the cancer. New treatments dealing with biopsies, stem cells, and therapy drugs that are being tested in clinical trials are also discussed. The National Cancer Institute is part of the National Institutes of Health and is the primary government agency for cancer research and information.

Different types of treatment are available for patients with breast cancer. Some treatments are standard (the currently used treatment), and some are being tested in clinical trials. Before starting treatment, patients may want to think about taking part in a clinical trial. A treatment clinical trial is a research

SOURCE: National Cancer Institute, "Breast Cancer Treatment," July 19, 2007. www.cancer.gov.

study meant to help improve current treatments or obtain information on new treatments for patients with cancer. When clinical trials show that a new treatment is better than the standard treatment, the new treatment may become the standard treatment. . . .

Four types of standard treatment are used.

Surgery

Most patients with breast cancer have surgery to remove the cancer from the breast. Some of the lymph nodes under the arm are usually taken out and looked at under a microscope to see if they contain cancer cells.

Breast-conserving surgery, an operation to remove the cancer but not the breast itself, includes the following:

Two types of breast surgery are shown in this illustration. The top diagram shows an invasive lumpectomy and the lower a modified radical mastectomy. (**Nucleus Medical Art, Inc./Alamy**)

Minimally Invasive Lumpectomy

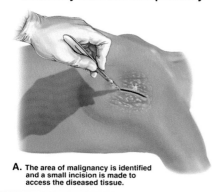

A. The area of malignancy is identified and a small incision is made to access the diseased tissue.

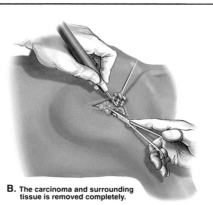

B. The carcinoma and surrounding tissue is removed completely.

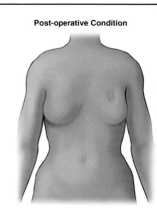

Post-operative Condition

Modified Radical Mastectomy

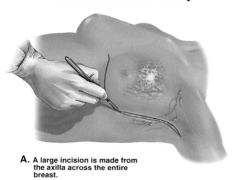

A. A large incision is made from the axilla across the entire breast.

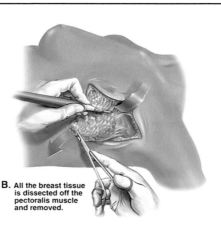

B. All the breast tissue is dissected off the pectoralis muscle and removed.

Post-operative Condition

- Lumpectomy: Surgery to remove a tumor (lump) and a small amount of normal tissue around it.
- Partial mastectomy: Surgery to remove the part of the breast that has cancer and some normal tissue around it. This procedure is also called a segmental mastectomy.

Patients who are treated with breast-conserving surgery may also have some of the lymph nodes under the arm removed for biopsy. This procedure is called a lymph node dissection. It may be done at the same time as the breast-conserving surgery or after. Lymph node dissection is done through a separate incision.

Other types of surgery include the following:

- Total mastectomy: Surgery to remove the whole breast that has cancer. This procedure is also called a simple mastectomy. Some of the lymph nodes under the arm may be removed for biopsy at the same time as the breast surgery or after. This is done through a separate incision.
- Modified radical mastectomy: Surgery to remove the whole breast that has cancer, many of the lymph nodes under the arm, the lining over the chest muscles, and sometimes, part of the chest wall muscles.
- Radical mastectomy: Surgery to remove the breast that has cancer, chest wall muscle under the breast, and all of the lymph nodes under the arm. This procedure is sometimes called a Halsted radical mastectomy.

Even if the doctor removes all the cancer that can be seen at the time of the surgery, some patients may be given radiation therapy, chemotherapy, or hormone therapy after surgery to kill any cancer cells that are left. Treatment given after the surgery, to increase the chances of a cure, is called adjuvant therapy.

If a patient is going to have a mastectomy, breast reconstruction (surgery to rebuild a breast's shape after a mastectomy) may be considered. Breast reconstruction may be done at the time of the mastectomy or at a future time. The reconstructed breast may be made with the patient's own (nonbreast) tissue or by using implants filled with saline or silicone gel. . . .

Radiation Therapy

Radiation therapy is a cancer treatment that uses high-energy x-rays or other types of radiation to kill cancer cells or keep them from growing. There are two types of radiation therapy. External radiation therapy uses a machine outside the body to send radiation toward the cancer. Internal radiation therapy uses a radioactive substance sealed in needles, seeds, wires, or catheters that are placed directly into or near the cancer. The way the radiation therapy is given depends on the type and stage of the cancer being treated.

> **FAST FACT**
>
> As many as 20 percent of patients suffer cardiac side effects from breast cancer treatments.

Chemotherapy

Chemotherapy is a cancer treatment that uses drugs to stop the growth of cancer cells, either by killing the cells or by stopping them from dividing. When chemotherapy is taken by mouth or injected into a vein or muscle, the drugs enter the bloodstream and can reach cancer cells throughout the body (systematic chemotherapy). When chemotherapy is placed directly into the spinal column, an organ, or a body cavity such as the abdomen, the drugs mainly affect cancer cells in those areas (regional chemotherapy). The way the chemotherapy is given depends on the type and stage of the cancer being treated.

Hormone Therapy

Hormone therapy is a cancer treatment that removes hormones or blocks their action and stops cancer cells

Breast Cancer Treatment Strategy Chart

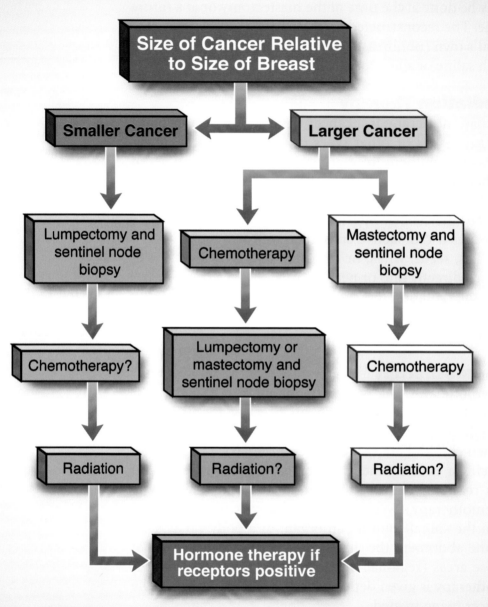

Note: This is a road map for the general sequencing of surgery, chemotherapy, and radiation. Individual patients can have special circumstances that require individual modifications of this sequence.

Taken from: David Chan, *Breast Cancer: Real Questions, Real Answers.* New York: Marlowe, 2006, p. 146.

from growing. Hormones are substances produced by glands in the body and circulated in the bloodstream. Some hormones can cause certain cancers to grow. If tests show that the cancer cells have places where hormones can attach (receptors), drugs, surgery, or radiation therapy are used to reduce the production of hormones or block them from working.

Hormone therapy with tamoxifen is often given to patients with early stages of breast cancer and those with metastatic breast cancer (cancer that has spread to other parts of the body). Hormone therapy with tamoxifen or estrogens can act on cells all over the body and may increase the chance of developing endometrial cancer. Women taking tamoxifen should have a pelvic exam every year to look for any signs of cancer. Any vaginal bleeding, other than menstrual bleeding, should be reported to a doctor as soon as possible.

Hormone therapy with an aromatase inhibitor is given to some postmenopausal women who have hormone-dependent breast cancer. Hormone-dependent breast cancer needs the hormone estrogen to grow. Aromatase inhibitors decrease the body's estrogen by blocking an enzyme called aromatase from turning androgen into estrogen.

For the treatment of early stage breast cancer, certain aromatase inhibitors may be used as adjuvant therapy instead of tamoxifen or after 2 or more years of tamoxifen. For the treatment of metastatic breast cancer, aromatase inhibitors are being tested in clinical trials to compare to hormone therapy with tamoxifen.

Four Types of Clinical Trials

New types of treatment are being tested in clinical trials. These include the following:

Sentinel lymph node biopsy followed by surgery. Sentinel lymph node biopsy is the removal of the sentinel lymph node during surgery. The sentinel lymph node is the first lymph node to receive lymphatic drainage from a tumor. It is the first lymph node the cancer is likely to spread to from the tumor. A radioactive substance and/or blue dye is injected near the tumor. The substance or dye flows through the lymph ducts to the lymph nodes. The first lymph node to receive the substance or dye is removed. A pathologist views the tissue under a microscope to look for cancer cells. If cancer cells are not found, it may not be necessary to remove more lymph nodes. After the sentinel lymph node biopsy, the surgeon removes the tumor (breast-conserving surgery or mastectomy).

High-dose chemotherapy with stem cell transplant. High-dose chemotherapy with stem cell transplant is a way of giving high doses of chemotherapy and replacing blood-forming cells destroyed by the cancer treatment. Stem cells (immature blood cells) are removed from the blood or bone marrow of the patient or a donor and are frozen and stored. After the chemotherapy is completed, the stored stem cells are thawed and given back to the patient through an infusion. These reinfused stem cells grow into (and restore) the body's blood cells.

Studies have shown that high-dose chemotherapy followed by stem cell transplant does not work better than standard chemotherapy in the treatment of breast cancer. Doctors have decided that, for now, high-dose chemotherapy should be tested only in clinical trials. Before taking part in such a trial, women should talk with their doctors about the serious side effects, including death, that may be caused by high-dose chemotherapy.

Monoclonal antibodies as adjuvant therapy. Monoclonal antibody therapy is a cancer treatment that uses antibodies made in the laboratory, from a single type of immune system cell. These antibodies can identify substances on cancer cells or normal substances that may help cancer cells grow. The antibodies attach to the substances and kill the cancer cells, block their growth, or keep them from spreading. Monoclonal antibodies are given by infusion. They may be used alone or to carry drugs, toxins, or radioactive material directly to cancer cells. Monoclonal antibodies are also used in combination with chemotherapy as adjuvant therapy.

Trastuzumab (Herceptin) is a monoclonal antibody that blocks the effects of the growth factor protein HER2, which transmits growth signals to breast cancer cells. About one-fourth of patients with breast cancer have tumors that may be treated with trastuzumab combined with chemotherapy.

Tyrosine kinase inhibitors as adjuvant therapy. Tyrosine kinase inhibitors are targeted therapy drugs that block signals needed for tumors to grow. Tyrosine kinase inhibitors may be used in combination with other anticancer drugs as adjuvant therapy.

Lapatinib is a tyrosine kinase inhibitor that blocks the effects of the HER2 protein and other proteins inside tumor cells. It may be used to treat patients with HER2-positive breast cancer that has progressed following treatment with trastuzumab.

Men and Breast Cancer

Teresa G. Odle

In the following article Teresa G. Odle discusses the rare condition of male breast cancer. While this type of cancer occurs more frequently in women because they have more breast tissue and cells, it can be very serious when occurring in men. The less common type of male breast cancer, along with less common conditions, are described. Also discussed are the causes, symptoms, diagnosis, and treatment options. According to the authors, there is a distinct lack of information regarding this subject, so men should be aware of the possibilities of this disease. Odle is a science and health writer for a variety of reference publications.

Breast cancer is rare in men, but can be serious and fatal. Many people believe that only women can get breast cancer, but men have breast tissue that also can develop cancer. When men and women are born, they have a small amount of breast tissue with a

SOURCE: Teresa G. Odle, "Male Breast Cancer," *The Gale Encyclopedia of Cancer: A Guide to Cancer and Its Treatments,* 2005. Reproduced by permission of Gale, a part of Cengage Learning.

few tubular passages called ducts located under the nipple and the area around the nipple (areola). By puberty, female sex hormones cause breast ducts to grow and milk glands to form at the ends of the ducts. But male hormones eventually prevent further breast tissue growth. Although male breast tissue still contains some ducts, it will have only a few—or no—lobules. Near the breasts of men and women are axillary lymph nodes. These are underarm small structures shaped like beans that collect cells from lymphatic vessels. Lymphatic vessels carry lymph, a clear fluid that contains fluid from tissues, cells from the immune system, and various waste products throughout the body. The axillary lymph nodes are important to breast cancer patients, as they play a role in the spread and staging of breast cancer.

Breast cancer is much more common in women, mostly because women have many more breast cells that can undergo cancerous changes and because women are exposed to the effects of female hormones.

Ductal Carcinoma

Infiltrating ductal carcinoma is the most common type of breast cancer in men. It is a type of adenocarcinoma, or a type of cancer that occurs in glandular tissue. Infiltrating ductal carcinoma starts in a breast duct and spreads beyond the cells lining the ducts to other tissues in the breast. Once the cancer begins spreading into the breast it can spread to other parts of the body. This distant spread is called metastasis. When breast cancer metastasizes to other areas of the body, it can cause serious, life-threatening consequences. For example, breast cancer might spread to the liver or lungs. About 80% to 90% of all male breast cancers are infiltrating ductal carcinomas.

Ductal carcinoma in situ (DCIS) is not common; it accounts for about 10% of all male breast cancers. It also is an adenocarcinoma. In situ cancers remain in the immediate area where they began, so DCIS remains confined to the breast ducts and does not spread to the fatty tissues of the breast. This means it is likely found early. DCIS also may be called intraductal carcinoma.

Other Carcinomas

Other types of breast cancer are very rare in men. Adeno-carcinomas that are lobular (forming in the milk glands or lobules) only occur in about 2% of male breast cancer cases because men normally do not have milk gland tissues. Inflammatory breast cancer, a serious form of breast cancer in which the breast looks red and swollen and feels warm, also occurs rarely. Paget's disease of the nipple, a type of breast cancer that grows from the ducts beneath the nipple onto the nipple's surface, only accounts for about 1% of female breast cancers. However, slightly more men have this form of breast cancer than women. Sometimes, Paget's disease is associated with another form of breast cancer.

Although not a form of cancer, but a benign condition, gynecomastia is important to mention. It is the most common of all male breast disorders and can be associated with male breast cancer in a rare condition called Klinefelter's syndrome. Gynecomastia most often occurs in teenage boys when their hormones change during puberty. Older men also may experience the condition when their hormone balance changes as they age. Gynecomastia is an increase in the amount of breast tissue, or breast tissue enlargement. If a man has Klinefelter's syndrome, he can develop gynecomastia and increased risk of breast cancer.

Demographics

Breast cancer in men is rare, accounting for less than 1% of all breast cancers. Still, about 1,450 American men were diagnosed with the disease and 470 men died from it in 2004. Although studies show the number of breast cancer cases in women has decreased in the United States

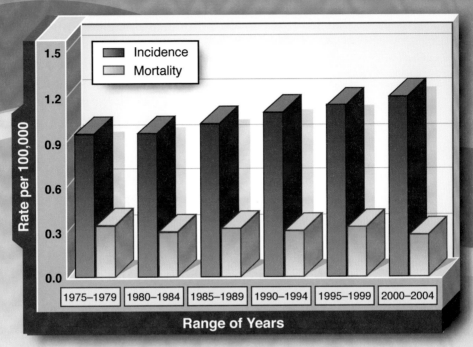

Trends in Male Breast Cancer Incidence

Taken from: American Cancer Society Surveillance Research, 2007.

and Europe since the 1960s, the number of breast cancer cases in men has not decreased, but remained stable or slightly increased.

The rate of increase in cases begins and steadily rises at age 50 for men. However, the average age for male breast cancer is between 60 and 70 years old, with a median age of 67 years. Men often are diagnosed at a later stage than women.

Causes

Scientists do not know what causes most cases of male breast cancer. However, excellent progress is being made in genetic research and in understanding how genes instruct cells to grow, divide, and die. . . . Genes are part of the body's DNA, which is the chemical that instructs the cells. When DNA or genes carry defects (mutations), they activate changes in the cells, such as rapid cell division, that lead to cancer. Some genes, called tumor suppression genes, cause cells to die. Scientists have identified some genetic mutations that are risk factors for breast cancer. In other cases, environmental, or outside, factors are thought to increase a man's risk for breast cancer.

Mutations of at least two versions of a tumor suppressor gene (BRCA1 and BRCA2) have been identified as causes of breast cancer in women. In men, the BRCA2 mutation is considered responsible for about 15% of breast cancers. Men can inherit genes from either parent. Studies have shown that BRCA1 also may increase a man's risk for breast cancer, but its role is less certain. These mutations have been shown to increase other cancers in men, including prostate cancer. Klinefelter's syndrome is a rare genetic cause of breast cancer in men. It results from inheriting an additional X chromosome.

Several other factors also may cause male breast cancer. Some conditions, such as the liver disease cirrhosis, can cause an imbalance in a man's hormones, producing high levels of the female hormone estrogen, which can lead to breast cancer. Exposure to some substances such as high amounts of radiation may contribute to male breast cancer. A 2004 report studied why a cluster of breast cancer cases occurred among a small group of men who worked in the basement office of a multi-story office building. The study linked their breast cancer to exposure to high magnetic fields from a nearby electrical switchgear room in their work space.

Symptoms

Many men do not realize they can develop breast cancer; they ignore the symptoms. The most common symptom is a mass, or lump in the chest area, particularly around the nipple. The lump will be firm, not tender or painful. Other signs that may warn of male breast cancer include:

- Skin dimpling or puckering
- Changes in the nipple, such as drawing inward (retraction)
- Nipple discharge of any kind
- Redness or scaling of the nipple or breast skin
- Abnormal swelling (or lump) of the breast nipple, or chest muscle
- Prolonged rash or irritation of the nipple, which may indicate Paget's disease

Diagnosis

Physicians follow the same steps for diagnosing breast cancer in men as in women, except that routine screening of breast cancer is not done in men. Once symptoms are noticed, however, physicians will proceed in the same way. The physician will conduct a thorough medical history and examination, including questions that may identify risk factors for breast cancer, such as male or female relatives with the disease. The medical history also helps gather details on possible symptoms for breast cancer. . . .

The next step in diagnosis usually is a diagnostic mammogram. Mammography is an x-ray of the breast. . . . If the initial mammogram shows suspicious findings, the radiologist may order magnification views to more closely look at the suspicious area. Mammograms can accurately show the tissue in the breast, even more so in men than women, because men do not have dense breasts or benign cysts in their breasts that interfere with the diagnosis.

The radiologist also might recommend an ultrasound to follow up on suspicious findings. Ultrasound often is used to image the breasts. Also known as sonography, the technique uses high-frequency sound waves to take pictures of organs and functions in the body. Sound wave echoes can be converted by computer to an image and displayed on a computer screen. Ultrasound does not use radiation. . . .

Biopsies, which involve removing a sample of tissue, are the only definite way to tell if a mass is cancerous. At one time, surgical biopsies were the only option, requiring removal of all or a large portion of the lump in a more complicated procedure. Today, fine-needle aspiration biopsy and core biopsies can be performed. In fine-needle aspiration biopsy, a thin needle is inserted to withdraw fluid from the mass. The physician may use ultrasound or other imaging guidance to locate the mass if necessary. The fluid is tested in a laboratory under a special microscope to determine if it is cancerous.

A core biopsy is similar, but involves removing a small cylinder of tissue from the mass through a slightly larger needle. Core biopsy may require local anesthesia. These biopsy techniques usually can be performed in a physician's office or outpatient facility. The cells in biopsy samples help physicians determine if the lump is cancerous and the type of breast cancer. A tissue sample also may be used for assigning a grade to the cancer and to test for certain proteins and receptors that aid in treatment and prognosis decisions.

If there is discharge from the nipple, the fluid also may be collected and analyzed in a laboratory to see if cancer cells are present in the fluid.

Diagnosis of breast cancer spread may require additional tests. For example, a computed tomography (CT) scan may be ordered to check organs such as the liver or kidney for possible metastasized cancer. A chest x-ray can initially check for cancer spread to the lungs. Bone scans are nuclear medicine procedures that look for areas of diseased bone. Magnetic resonance imaging (MRI) has been increasingly used in recent years as a follow-up study to mammograms when findings are not clear. However, for metastatic breast cancer, they are more likely to be ordered to check for cancer in the brain and spinal cord. Positron emission tomography (PET) scans also have become more common in recent years. . . .

Staging

Cancer staging systems help physicians compare treatments and research and identify patients for clinical trials. Most of all, they help physicians determine treatment and prognosis for individual patients by describing how severe a patient's cancer is in relation to the primary tumor. The most common system used for cancer is the American Joint Committee on Cancer (AJCC) TNM system, which bases staging largely on the spread of the cancer. T stands for tumor and describes the tumor's size and spread locally, or within the breast and to nearby organs. The letter N stands for lymph nodes and describes the cancer's possible spread to and within the lymph node system. . . . M stands for metastasis to note if the cancer has spread to distant organs. Further letters and numbers may follow these three letters to describe number of lymph nodes involved, approximate tumor sizes, or other information. . . .

Treatment Options

If the axillary lymph nodes were identified as containing cancer at the time of the sentinel lymph node biopsy, they will be removed in an axillary dissection. Sometimes, this is done at the time of the biopsy.

For Stage I, surgery often is the only treatment needed for men. Women often have lumpectomies, which remove as little surrounding breast tissue as possible, to preserve some of their breast shape. For men, this is less of a concern, and mastectomy, or removal of the breast, is performed in 80% of all male breast cancers. Men with Stage I tumors larger than 1 cm may receive additional (adjuvant) chemotherapy.

Men with Stage II breast cancer also usually receive a mastectomy. If they have cancer in the lymph nodes, they probably will receive adjuvant therapy. Those with estrogen receptor–positive tumors may receive hormone therapy with tamoxifen. The treatment team may recommend adjuvant radiation therapy if the cancer has spread to nearby lymph nodes and/or to the skin.

Stage III breast cancer requires mastectomy followed by adjuvant therapy with tamoxifen when hormones are involved. Most patients with Stage III disease also will require chemotherapy and radiation therapy to the chest wall.

Men with Stage IV breast cancer will require systemic therapy, or chemotherapy and perhaps hormonal therapy that works throughout the body to fight the cancer in the breast, as well as the cancer cells that have spread. Patients also may receive immunotherapy to help fight

Male breast cancer accounts for only 1 percent of all breast cancers. The standard treatment is a mastectomy. (Norman Price/Alamy)

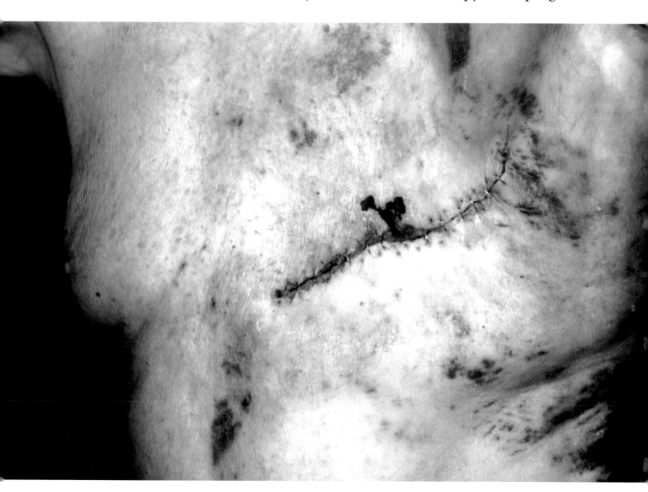

infection following chemotherapy. Radiation and surgery also may be used to relieve symptoms of the primary cancer and areas where the cancer may have spread. The treatment team also may have to diagnose specific treatments for the metastatic cancers, depending on their sites.

If male breast cancer recurs in the breast or chest wall, it can be treated with surgical removal and followed by radiation therapy. An exception is recurrence in the same area, where additional radiation therapy can damage normal tissue. Recurrence of the cancer in distant sites is treated the same as metastases found at the time of diagnosis.

Prognosis

Prognosis for male breast cancer varies, depending on stage. Generally, prognosis is poorer for men than for women, because men tend to show up for diagnosis when their breast cancer has reached a later stage. The average five-year survival rate for Stage I cancers is 96%. For Stage II, it is 84%. Stage III cancers carry an average five-year survival rate of 52%, and by Stage IV, the rate drops to 24%.

Alternative and Complementary Therapies

Many alternative and complementary therapies can help cancer patients relax and deal with pain, though none to date have been shown to treat or prevent male breast cancer. For example, traditional Chinese medicine offers therapies that stress the importance of balancing energy forces. Many studies also show that guided imagery, prayer, meditation, laughter, and a positive approach to cancer can help promote healing. Early studies have shown that soy and flaxseed may have some preventive properties for breast cancer. However, these trials have been conducted in women. When looking for these therapies, cancer support groups suggest asking for credible referrals and working with the medical treatment team to coordinate alternative and complementary care. . . .

Prevention

Some forms of male breast cancer cannot be prevented. But detecting the cancer at an early stage can prevent serious complications, such as spread to distant organs. Men who have a history of breast cancer in their family should pay particular attention to the symptoms of breast cancer and seek immediate medical evaluation. Physicians may be able to test the blood of men with family history for presence of the BRCA2 gene so they may more carefully watch for early signs of breast cancer. Avoiding exposure to radiation also may help prevent some male breast cancers.

Men should remember that there are important differences between male and female breast cancers. Some experts say that specific guidelines and instructions for men with breast cancer are noticeably lacking, so men should not be afraid to ask questions or to push a physician for more information when he suspects he might have a suspicious lump or finding in his breast.

Breast Cancer in Young Women

Susan M. Love with Karen Lindsey

In the following selection Susan M. Love discusses the problems associated with breast cancer in young women. One of the concerns is heredity. If a woman is predisposed to breast cancer, she is more likely to contract it at a younger age. But the majority of young women who have breast cancer have no family history of the disease. According to Love, another major concern with young women and breast cancer is reproduction. Treatments can interfere with a woman's fertility, which is not necessarily a problem for older patients, but is a major concern for young women battling the disease. Love also discusses the importance of support groups for young women. Love is president and medical director of the Dr. Susan Love Research Foundation, a nonprofit breast cancer organization, and is a director of the National Breast Cancer Coalition. Karen Lindsey writes about medical topics and feminist issues.

SOURCE: Susan M. Love with Karen Lindsey, *Dr. Susan Love's Breast Book*. Cambridge, MA: Da Capo Press, 2005. Copyright © 2005 by Susan M. Love, M.D. All rights reserved. Reprinted by permission of De Capo Press, a member of Perseus Books, L.L.C.

Sometimes cancer occurs in an unusual situation. . . . Breast cancer is most common in women over 50, and there are many cases in women in their 40s. It's far more rare in women under 40, but it does occur. We tend to be particularly shocked when it occurs in a young woman. Usually in this situation it's detected as a lump, since we generally don't do screening mammography in young women. . . .

Often a young woman gets misdiagnosed. She detects a lump or a thickening, and she's told it's just lumpy breasts, or "fibrocystic disease," and it's followed for a while until doctors realize it's serious. The vast majority of lumps in women under 35 are benign, and the risk of cancer is very low. Still, it's important for doctors to be vigilant and bear in mind that young women can develop breast cancer.

The youngest patient I ever diagnosed was 23. She was on her honeymoon and discovered a lump. We diagnosed her as having cancer; she had a positive node, and she underwent radiation and chemotherapy. Ten years later she developed a local recurrence that required a mastectomy.

FAST FACT

Five percent of all breast cancer cases occur in women under the age of forty.

The Conditions of Breast Cancer in Young Women

Breast cancer in younger women is more likely to be hereditary. If you've inherited a mutation (and you need only one or two more mutations to get cancer), you're one step closer and likely to get there faster, whereas if you "acquire" breast cancer, you still need to get all of the mutations. That doesn't work all the time. Like older women, the majority of younger women with breast cancer have no family history. But if you have breast cancer in your family you're more likely to get it at a younger age than if you don't.

Many doctors believe that breast cancer in a young woman is more aggressive than in older ones. Two studies shed some light on this theory. Both show that the mortality from breast cancer is higher in women who have been pregnant in the past four years. The risk is highest right after a pregnancy and decreases with each year, going back to normal after four years. This makes sense, since pregnancy affects both the milk duct lining cells, making them divide more, and the local environment. Since young women are more likely to have been recently pregnant (25 percent of all breast cancers in women younger than 35 are associated with pregnancy), they show more of this effect. This suggests that it may

Many doctors believe that breast cancer in younger women is more aggressive than in older women. (**Bob Pardue/Alamy**)

not be the woman's age itself that affects aggressiveness but the changes in her immune system (necessary so that her body won't reject the fetus) and in the hormones that go with pregnancy.

Overall, there is no evidence that breast cancer in a woman under 35 matched for prognostic features is any more aggressive than a cancer in an older woman. Younger women do, however, have a higher incidence of poor prognostic features such as negative estrogen receptors, poor differentiation, and high proliferative (growth) rates. Still, a young woman and an older woman with the same tumors have the same general prognosis.

Treatment Questions

With younger women, there's some question about whether it's safe to do lumpectomy and radiation. The concern is twofold. One is that we don't know what the long-term (40- to 60-year) risks of radiation are. The other is that there appears to be a higher local recurrence rate reported in young women who get lumpectomy and radiation than in women in their 40s and 50s. However, recent studies show that there's also a higher local recurrence after mastectomy in that group. The treatment for breast cancer in young women is pretty much the same as for older women, with the option of either breast conservation surgery with radiation or mastectomy with or without reconstruction.

Interestingly, chemotherapy works better in younger than in older women. We've decreased the death rate for breast cancer through treatment in this subgroup more than in any other. There are problems with chemotherapy, however. Often it puts a young woman into menopause. The really young woman—in her 20s or early 30s—is less likely to have that happen than the woman in her late 30s or early 40s. The closer you are to your natural menopause the more likely it is to push you over. This also varies according to the chemotherapy drugs you take. The

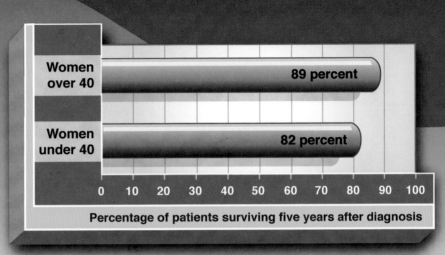

Cancer Survival Rates by Age

Women over 40 — 89 percent

Women under 40 — 82 percent

0 10 20 30 40 50 60 70 80 90 100

Percentage of patients surviving five years after diagnosis

Taken from: American Cancer Society.

much younger woman will probably get her period back after the treatment course is finished. There is considerable controversy as to whether this is a good thing or not. Some data suggest that a premenopausal woman who is still menstruating postchemotherapy and is sensitive to estrogen may benefit from two to three years of temporary menopause.

Fertility Issues

A web-based survey of young women with breast cancer revealed, not surprisingly, that fertility after treatment was a major concern. Because of the likelihood of chemotherapy-induced menopause, some women have considered preserving their eggs before the treatment so they can still have children later. There are problems with that, however. With the current state of technology, you can save an embryo but not an egg. So you must choose your sperm donor or partner. While I was writing this edition, an exciting report came out from Dr. Kutluk Oktay at Cornell [University in New York State]. He was able to remove some ovarian tissue from a 30-year-old woman with breast cancer before she underwent chemotherapy which, as she had feared, resulted in menopause. Six years later he transplanted her frozen ovarian tissue and ovarian function resumed. He was able to harvest eggs and, with in vitro fertilization, one developed into a four-cell embryo in a petri dish. Whether she will actually be able to get pregnant and carry the embryo and fetus to term is unknown at this writing, but this is a first step toward preserving fertility in young women who need chemotherapy.

The second problem is that a lot of hormones must be administered to make the eggs grow for harvesting. Doctors are often reluctant to give those high doses of hormones to women who have had cancer, especially those with hormone receptor positive tumors. Attempts have been made to retrieve eggs without hormone stimulation, and recently tamoxifen has been used to help harvest eggs from 12 women prior to chemotherapy. Two of the women in the tamoxifen group and two of five women in the no-stimulation group conceived.

This is obviously a moving target. If this is an issue for you, make sure you check out your options before undergoing chemotherapy. And remember there are other ways to parent. Losing your fertility does not mean losing all chances to be a parent.

When a young woman has breast cancer, there's an increased risk for her mother, sisters, and daughters, and they should all be monitored closely.

Support for Young Women

Finding the right support group can be difficult for the younger woman, who can feel out of place among women in their 50s and older. . . . Most hospitals have support groups for young women because the issues they face are often quite different from older women's. There are several books on dating after mastectomy, which is a concern to single women of all ages, as are the psychosocial issues. . . .

The incidence of breast cancer in the other breast is about 0.8 percent per year, which usually maximizes out to about 10–15 percent. However, women with BRCA 1 or BRCA 2 (about 6 percent of women under 36) mutations can have a much higher chance of developing a second breast cancer in the same or other breast. Since younger women have many more years to get cancer in the opposite breast, their risk is slightly higher than that of older women. Both chemotherapy and hormone therapy reduce this risk.

The Future of Breast Cancer

Judith Cookis Rubens

In the following article Judith Cookis Rubens explains how improved screening methods, new drug therapies, and advanced surgical techniques are contributing to a decrease in breast cancer death rates. Rubens discusses advances in understanding the disease at the molecular level to improve drug therapies and new techniques in radiation therapy that allow women to decrease their treatment time by up to two-thirds. Also explained are new types of breast reconstruction that may allow women to retain more muscle. Rubens is a Michigan-based writer.

Breast cancer remains a scary, real health threat. But today, thanks to better screening tools, refined surgical techniques, and targeted drug and hormone therapies, a cancer diagnosis isn't so grim. Breast cancer death rates have fallen in the past 20 years, a fact experts link to earlier diagnoses and a move away from one-size-fits-all treatments. "The whole trend now is to do less surgery and more individualized treatment," says Cheryl Wesen, M.D., a breast surgeon and director of breast care services for St. John Health Systems. Here are some of the latest breakthroughs in the ongoing battle against breast cancer and in reconstructive treatment.

FAST FACT

One in five breast cancers may be missed by traditional mammography.

Accurate Detection

Doctors usually screen for breast cancer using mammography, which picks up about 80% to 90% of tumors in women without symptoms, the American Cancer Society [ACS] says. But mammography is advancing. More imaging centers are switching from film to digital mammography technology. Radiologists can enlarge suspicious areas on an electronic image more easily, and new computer-assisted diagnosis software flags trouble spots for doctors to re-check.

In early 2007, the ACS recommended annual MRIs (magnetic resonance imaging) plus mammograms for women 30 and older who are at high risk of developing breast cancer (those who have a strong family history of breast or ovarian cancer or who have been treated with radiation for Hodgkin's disease).

Some studies have shown breast MRIs are better at finding small aggressive tumors in women with dense breasts. The downside? They pick up so much that they cause false positives. "It's not the right test for every woman to have," says Wesen.

Treatment Advances

Identifying genetic predisposition for breast cancer by screening for the BRCA1 and BRCA2 genes was the big news of the last decade. Now scientists also better understand breast tumors at the molecular level and how hormone receptors work inside those cells.

A woman has her breast scanned by an MRI machine to detect any small tumors. (Phototake Inc./Alamy)

"We're improving our ability to do good molecular diagnosis so we know exactly which drugs to use in which setting," says Stephen Ethier, Ph.D., deputy director and associate center director for basic science at the Barbara Ann Karmanos Cancer Institute in Detroit. About 60% to 65% of patients have estrogen-receptor positive tumors, meaning anti-estrogen drugs such as tamoxifen can sometimes stop tumor growth, Ethier says. But for post-menopausal women with early-stage breast cancer, tamoxifen is no longer the gold standard. The latest results of several international trials showed that for these women, aromatase inhibitors, a new class of drugs that prevent cells from actually making estrogen, worked better than tamoxifen. Ethier says there is still some debate over which drugs are best.

For another one-quarter of patients with HER-2 positive tumors—an aggressive, fast-growing type—the drug of choice to slow recurrence has been trastuzumab (brand name Herceptin), an intravenous drug that didn't work for everyone. A next-generation pill called lapatinib (brand name Tykerb) looks more potent in clinical testing, Ethier says. It still attacks the HER-2 protein, but in a different way. "There are more of these kinds of new drugs to come," Ethier adds.

Radiation Advances

There are advances in radiation, too, such as new techniques in partial breast irradiation for women with early cancer. Instead of Monday through Friday treatments over six weeks, some new protocols deliver the same radiation dose in one to two weeks, Ethier says.

Also making news is the pricey genetic test Oncotype DX, which aims to tell women with early-stage cancer whether it will recur and whether they would benefit from intense chemotherapy.

"Three of four patients with zero positive lymph nodes are cured with surgery and radiation. Only one in four will recur with aggressive disease later on. The question is, 'How do you tell who's who?'" Ethier says. "This is a test that could not have even been imagined 10 to 15 years ago, let alone done."

Building a Better Breast

Someday, experts say, we won't need to talk about radical or total mastectomy. Until then, for those considering reconstruction, there are new types of silicone gel implants that offer a natural softness and shape, and are less likely to leak outside the pocket where the implant is placed, should the implant rupture, says Edwin G. Wilkins, M.D., a plastic surgeon specializing in mastectomy reconstruction at the University of Michigan Health System in Ann Arbor.

Mind-body	Soy supplements
Massage	Essiac tea
Acupuncture	Black cohosh
_____	Large doses of vitamins A and C

Taken from: Harvard Special Health Report, "Complementary and Alternative Therapies: Breast Cancer," 2004.

"The newest generation of gels aren't the liquid silicone that people remember," Wilkins says.

About half of Wilkins' patients choose implants during reconstruction, but the other half choose to rebuild the breast using their own tissue. The standard TRAM flap surgery, which uses pieces of abdominal wall muscle, left women with reduced sit-up power. Newer techniques—known as DIEP or GAP flap surgeries—use lower abdominal skin and fat or buttock skin and fat, but no muscle, to build the new breast.

"Moving tissue without sacrificing muscle is the new frontier," Wilkins says.

More Survivors

One in eight women will be diagnosed with breast cancer during her lifetime. That's the bad news: The lifetime risk has gradually increased over the past 30 years, in part due to longer life expectancies. But the good news is many women are also surviving longer with cancer. The all-important five-year survival rate for breast cancers diagnosed from 1996–2003 was 88.6%, up from 86% between 1992–97, the National Cancer Institute reports.

"Finding a cure for breast cancer is everybody's primary goal," says [University of Michigan's] Wilkins.

CHAPTER 2

The Controversial Side of Breast Cancer

Estrogen Is Beneficial to Breast Health

Dixie Mills

In this selection Dixie Mills explains that the exact causes of breast cancer are currently not known, and the exact workings of estrogen in the breast tissue are also unknown. While estrogen has been linked to breast cancer through hormone replacement therapy, studies have not shown how some hormones are chemically changed in a woman's body. Another issue with estrogen is that it is often not separated into its different formulas for study. Many women react to differing types of estrogen in varying ways, states Mills. Since a woman's estrogen production goes down with age, but breast cancer rates rise with age, Mills believes that other influences in the body are important in causing breast cancer. Mills cofounded the Breast Cancer High-Risk Clinic at the Dana-Farber Cancer Institute in Boston and is a member of the Association of Women Surgeons and the National Breast Cancer Coalition.

Photo on facing page.
An illustration shows plants that contain phytoestrogens. They are thought to ease menopausal symptoms and prevent osteoporosis and heart disease.
(Phototake Inc./Alamy)

SOURCE: Dixie Mills, "Causes of Breast Cancer—The Estrogen Controversy," *Women to Women*, November 28, 2007. Copyright © 2008. Reprinted from womentowomen.com with permission of Concordia Partners, L.L.C.

Noone knows what causes breast cancer, and no one can clearly say why we are seeing an increase in breast cancer cases. More women develop breast cancer than men—about 100 cases in females for every one in a man. Women's bodies make more estrogen than men's. Therefore, the conventional wisdom has been that estrogen causes breast cancer.

Some would label this guilt by association; many direct links are missing. One of the biggest missing links is that women's estrogen levels actually fall as they age, decreasing dramatically after menopause, but the incidence of breast cancer increases with age. The risk ratio that we all hear about—that one in eight women get breast cancer—is for women over 90 years of age. The rate for women in their 50's is more like one in 50.

So obviously there is much more than estrogen going on in the development of breast cancer, and it is being over-simplistic to think of estrogen as a bad poison when it comes to breast health. Estrogen is a very beneficial hormone in general—it stimulates tissues to grow when we need it to, and it is also a helpful player in response to stress. Let's explore what we know about the causes of breast cancer, what we don't know, and what this may mean for you.

Hormones and Breast Cancer

What we don't know, but researchers are studying, is how estrogen works in the breast tissue. We now realize that estrogen is probably secreted or produced directly from breast tissue—some from the fat of the breast, some from the ducts themselves. How and why this production continues throughout life is unknown. We also now realize that the body has many self-regulating or balancing mechanisms—that one hormone is usually balanced by another.

In the uterus the estrogen that stimulates the uterus to grow is then balanced by progesterone which stops it.

Unfortunately the mechanism may not be so simple in the breast. Breast and uterus are two very different tissues and the breast does not shed its lining once a month, but I still think the body works by self-regulating in some way.

Hormone Replacement Therapy

Provera—a synthetic progestin (the natural compound was changed to make it patentable)—has been shown to increase breast cancer risk in several studies, and appears to be the bad actor in Prempro in the Women's Health Initiative study. (Prempro is a combination of Premarin and Provera, both synthetics.) Why a small change in the synthetic compound should make this big a difference is confusing and distressing and needs more attention. However, natural progesterone has just not been studied that well.

There are definitive studies that bolster the connection between HRT [hormone replacement therapy] with high doses of progestins and a reoccurrence of breast cancer. One trial, the HABITS (Hormonal Replacement Therapy After Breast Cancer—Is It Safe?), was stopped at the median follow-up because the risk of reoccurrence was 3.3 times higher than in women receiving no treatment or HRT with low-dose progestin.

In another study on progesterone and menopause, researchers compared the effects of topical progesterone cream to prescribed oral progesterone on a small group of 12 healthy post-menopausal women. Data revealed that the OTC [over-the-counter] progesterone cream resulted in similar progesterone blood levels as the prescribed oral form. The women also had the same rate of adverse side effects. The complete results of the study were published in the June 2005 *Journal of Clinical Pharmacology.*

> **FAST FACT**
>
> In addition to reducing menopausal symptoms, estrogen protects bone density and prevents diabetes.

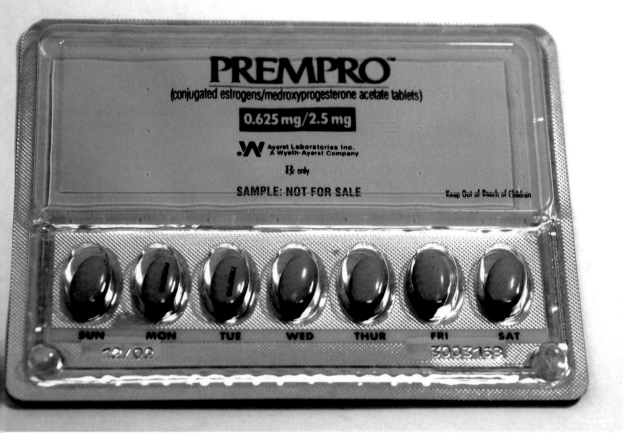

PREMPRO™
(conjugated estrogens/medroxyprogesterone acetate tablets)

0.625 mg/2.5 mg

Ayerst Laboratories Inc.
A Wyeth-Ayerst Company

℞ only

SAMPLE: NOT FOR SALE   Keep Out of Reach of Children

SUN   MON   TUE   WED   THUR   FRI   SAT

Controversy over the hormone replacement drug Prempro's increasing the risk of breast cancer prompted the National Institutes of Health to recommend women be taken off the drug. (Frances Roberts/Alamy)

What this tells us is that we still don't fully understand how progesterone is metabolized in our bodies or how the pathway changes as we age.

One thing we do know is that nature did not intend for women to maintain high levels of progesterone after menopause. Artificially doing so may pose additional health risks depending on your health history. Consequently, we don't recommend using progesterone of any kind for more than 12 months if you're post-menopausal.

The Complexities of Estrogen

Another big problem is that all estrogen is lumped together as one entity—but estrogen made by human ovaries is different from a pregnant mare's (the type used in Premarin), as well as the estrogens from plants (phytoestrogens) or environmental estrogens from breakdown products of chemicals in pesticides or cosmetics (xenoestrogens). These xenoestrogens may play a critical role, as they boost effective estrogen levels above normal levels and interfere in unknown ways with estrogen metabolism.

The fundamental structure of estrogen, for those who remember basic biology, is a steroid ring which can have different carbon and hydrogen molecules attached. These little differences between our estrogen and synthetics or xenoestrogens can confuse the body and create havoc. . . .

There were some women in the WHI [Women's Health Initiative] study who tolerated Premarin, which is a much stronger estrogen than the body is used to, without problems—their bodies metabolized it, used it, and then excreted it without obvious difficulty. Other women didn't like how the synthetic hormones made them feel and stopped using them. For others, something stimulated their breasts to make cancer cells. But what we don't know is what caused that errant growth, how or why. Do certain women have a genetic error that doesn't let them process synthetic estrogens or xenoestrogens? We just don't know—so the NIH [National Institutes of Health] decided it was safer to take all women off Prempro and Premarin because of the increased risk of breast cancer and other serious diseases. They are still investigating the difference between Premarin and bioidentical estrogens. We do not know if bioidentical hormones also increase the risk. There is no evidence that they do, and we believe because they are more natural that they are safer than synthetic hormones, but frankly, more study is needed.

I have had a few patients who developed breast cancer while using "natural" hormones. However, the vast majority of women who use these bioidentical forms feel that their quality of life benefits outweigh any unknown risks.

Estrogen Metabolism

Another missing link in the blame-estrogen theory is that estrogen is not just one natural formula. There are at least three estrogens, known as E1, E2, and E3, or by the names estrone, estradiol, and estriol. Confusing? Yes —medical students learn this in about one hour in medical school, gynecologists learn a bit more in their training, but few really understand the differences. And wait, there's more—which is even less well understood by your doctor, unless she or he is a biochemist.

Estrogen is broken down into metabolites which are then excreted in your feces or urine. Some of these metabolites have been found to be more carcinogenic than others and their ratio may be the most important factor. Sound familiar? It reminds me of cholesterol—where we have the good type and the bad type and the ratio of the two is what matters. Estrogen metabolites can now be measured in the blood or the urine and different dietary maneuvers made to improve the ratio. These tests are just coming onto the scene in conventional doctors' offices.

We know from cell biology that most bodily processes require simple cofactors to keep things going. These cofactors are basic vitamins and minerals, some made by the body and others required from the diet. Our diets have drastically changed from our ancestors' and even our parents', and that is why we and the American Medical Association recommend a high-quality multivitamin for everyone.

The Study of Estrogen

Estrogen metabolism is not simple and has not been well studied. Unfortunately, women subjects were considered too difficult to use in many clinical trials of the past, primarily because their hormones just changed too much to be "standardized." . . .

Hopefully, with more women in medicine—half of medical students now are women—more attention will be paid to women's issues. And with computer technology data can be collected and tabulated with greater ease than in the past. But we need to keep asking the questions. You can ask your healthcare provider these ques-

Probabilities of Developing Breast Cancer by Age

If current age is:	The probability of developing breast cancer in the next 10 years is:	or 1 in:
20	0.05 percent	1,837
30	0.43 percent	234
40	1.43 percent	70
50	2.51 percent	40
60	3.51 percent	28
70	3.88 percent	26
Lifetime Risk:	**12.28 percent**	8

Taken from: American Cancer Society Breast Cancer Facts and Figures 2007–2008.

tions and preface it with, "I don't expect you to know the answer, but don't you find it interesting?"

It is my personal opinion, based on nearly two decades of practice, that it cannot be just estrogen but other factors in the body, using, balancing, controlling, or feeding estrogen which are key to the development of breast cancer.

The truth is that we're pretty early in the process of discovering the causes of breast cancer. At the moment what we know is modest compared to what we don't know. It's going to be complex—like women! Perhaps the answer is right in front of us and we just aren't wearing the right colored glasses to see it. But to blame estrogen may be unfair and even dangerous because we lose sight of the real culprit or culprits.

Estrogen Increases the Risk of Breast Cancer

Mary Jane Minkin and Toby Hanlon

Mary Jane Minkin and Toby Hanlon state in this viewpoint that estrogen and the progestin in hormone replacement therapy (HRT) are associated with a higher risk of breast cancer. Although there have been inconsistencies in studies surrounding HRT, estrogen has been consistently linked with an increase in the risk of breast cancer by at least 20 percent. Short-term use can be okay, but long-term use is not recommended. Mary Jane Minkin and Toby Hanlon are writers for *Prevention* magazine.

I'm in a panic over the two recent studies showing that the progestin in my HRT puts me at even greater risk for breast cancer than the estrogen does. Should I stop taking my hormones?

My office has been overwhelmed with phone calls from concerned women asking this same question. These new studies—one published in the January 26 issue of the *Journal*

SOURCE: Mary Jane Minkin and Toby Hanlon, "Breast Cancer and HRT: More Questions than Answers," *Prevention*, August 2000. Reproduced by permission.

of the American Medical Association (JAMA) and the other appearing in the February 16 [2000] issue of the *Journal of the National Cancer Institute (JNCI)*—still don't settle the controversies regarding breast cancer risk and postmenopausal hormone therapy. In fact, they raise more questions. But since you and millions of other women still need to make decisions today based on what we know, here's the way I look at it and what I'm telling my patients.

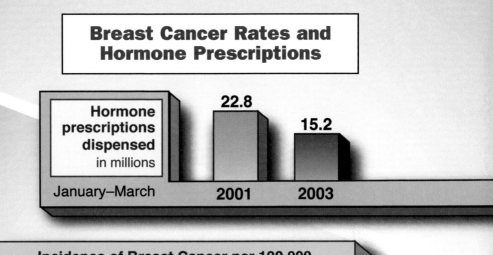

Breast Cancer Rates and Hormone Prescriptions

Hormone prescriptions dispensed in millions

22.8

15.2

January–March

2001

2003

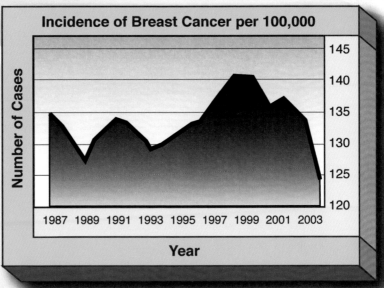

Incidence of Breast Cancer per 100,000

Number of Cases

145

140

135

130

125

120

1987 1989 1991 1993 1995 1997 1999 2001 2003

Year

Taken from: MSNBC, "Breast Cancer Drop Tied to Less Hormone Therapy," December 14, 2006. www.msnbc.msn.com.

Data sources are IMS Health, *Journal of the American Medical Association*, and the National Center for Health Statistics.

What These Findings Mean

Breast cancer is probably the biggest fear that women have when considering the risks and benefits of post-menopausal estrogen replacement therapy (ERT), even though there's no consensus on whether it causes breast cancer. Some studies show no increased risk for breast cancer. Others suggest there may be a slight increased risk, while still others say that there is an increased risk, but it's minimal and occurs only after 10 or more years of use.

Talk to the Doctor

Such inconsistent findings have led many experts—including me—to feel comfortable saying that any real increase in risk is probably very small or occurs in a very limited population.

Now we have two new [in 2000] studies suggesting that HRT—the combination of estrogen and a progestin—increases the risk for breast cancer even more than estrogen alone. (For a woman with a uterus, adding a progestin to estrogen therapy protects the endometrium from cell overgrowth and possible cancer.) There were hopes that the progestin would protect the breast from estrogen's effects. But based on the new findings, we can safely say that it doesn't.

How much increase in breast cancer risk was found? According to the *JAMA* study, taking estrogen alone for at least 4 years increased the risk for breast cancer by 20%. This means that the average woman's lifetime risk (that is, the risk of someone who doesn't have a family or genetic history of breast cancer) would increase from 12% to about 14%. Taking HRT increased the risk 40%, bringing a woman's lifetime risk to almost 17%. The *JNCI* study found a 24% increase in risk with every 5 years of HRT use.

There is some good news. The increased risk for breast cancer disappeared within 4 years of stopping the HRT.

Breast Cancer Rates of Women Who Use Hormone Replacement Therapy

A study found that taking a combination of estrogen and progestin pills to lessen menopausal symptoms may cause breast cancer and make it harder to detect at an early stage.

Study participants who took estrogen and progestin

Study participants who took a placebo

Number of Breast Cancer Cases

	Number of Participants	Number of Cases
	8,506	245
	8,102	185

Breast cancers that had spread by the time they were diagnosed:

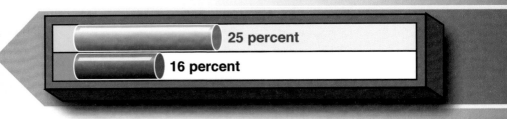

25 percent

16 percent

Taken from: *Journal of the American Medical Association*/AP Graphics.

Should I Give Up HRT?

Probably not. The benefits of HRT still outweigh the risks in my opinion. But you have to tailor your decisions to your individual needs as well as your anxieties. Here are some points to guide you:

Short-term use is okay. Both the *JAMA* and *JNCI* studies confirm that using ERT or HRT for less than 4 to 5 years does not increase the risk of breast cancer, which is consistent with other studies. So if you are taking either to relieve menopausal symptoms such as hot flashes, mood swings, or sleep disturbances, don't be afraid to continue. If you decide to use hormones longer, be aware that breast cancer risk may increase with duration of use.

Don't isolate the breast from the rest of the body. Estrogen offers proven bone protection, boosts life expectancy, and may protect your heart. It may even help prevent Alzheimer's disease and colon cancer.

But there are also other ways to prevent heart disease and osteoporosis, including regular exercise, a low-fat diet, certain other drugs, and not smoking. Decide what you want to protect most, and choose what best suits your risk factors.

Consider taking your progestin less frequently. One of the biggest complaints women have about certain HRT regimens is that they cause a monthly period again. Most women probably don't need to have a period every month. Taking progestin every other month or even every 3 months has been shown to be just as protective against endometrial cancer.

This doesn't mean that you can stop taking a progestin altogether, but you may want to discuss cutting back with your gynecologist.

FAST FACT

Obese women with a body mass index of 30 or above have been shown to have estrogen concentrations between 60 percent and 219 percent higher than women with a healthy BMI.

Abortion Raises the Risk of Breast Cancer

Coalition on Abortion/Breast Cancer

In the following selection the authors argue that abortion can have a significant impact on a woman's risk of developing breast cancer. According to the Coalition on Abortion/Breast Cancer, there are two risks involved. The recognized risk is that waiting to have a child at a later age extends the time that a woman's breasts have a majority of cancer-vulnerable breast tissue. The second risk, states the authors, is a debated risk regarding how much an abortion affects a woman's breast tissue. Also discussed are several studies that cite a link between abortion and breast cancer and the women who are associated with having a high risk of having this connection. The Coalition on Abortion/Breast Cancer provides education and information on the link between breast cancer and abortion.

Women have the right to know that two breast cancer risks are associated with abortion—a recognized risk and a debated risk.

SOURCE: "The ABC Link," Coalition on Abortion/Breast Cancer, May 30, 2007. Reproduced by permission.

The Recognized Breast Cancer Risk

All experts agree that the longer a woman waits to have her first full-term pregnancy, the greater her breast cancer risk is. Delaying the birth of a first child significantly increases risk because the childless woman has immature, cancer-vulnerable breast tissue—Type 1 and 2 lobules where 95% of all breast cancers are known to develop. Her breast tissue does not mature into cancer-resistant tissue until the last months of a full-term pregnancy. By the end of a 40-week pregnancy, 85% of her breast lobules are mature, cancer-resistant lobules known as Type 4 lobules.

A delayed first full-term pregnancy increases her risk because it extends the length of time during which her

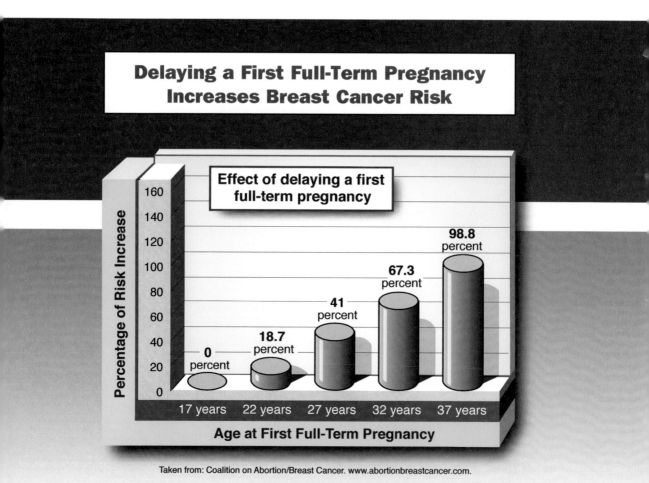

Delaying a First Full-Term Pregnancy Increases Breast Cancer Risk

Effect of delaying a first full-term pregnancy

Taken from: Coalition on Abortion/Breast Cancer. www.abortionbreastcancer.com.

breasts remain susceptible to carcinogens. Scientists define an early first full-term pregnancy as one that takes place before age 24.

Although delaying the birth of a first child is a known cancer risk, few experts have the intellectual honesty or the political courage to admit that abortion contributes to the breast cancer epidemic by causing a countless number of women to delay their first full-term pregnancies every year.

The Debated Breast Cancer Risk

Experts debate whether an abortion further increases risk by leaving the woman with more cancer-vulnerable breast tissue than she had before she became pregnant. This effect is known as the "independent link."

The breasts grow considerably during pregnancy while under the influence of high levels of the hormone estrogen, a known carcinogen. Estrogen causes the woman's normal and cancer-vulnerable breast lobules to multiply. If she has an abortion, she's left with more places for cancers to start in her breasts. If she has a baby, then other pregnancy hormones mature her breast lobules into cancer-resistant lobules during the last months of pregnancy. She's left with more cancer-resistant tissue than she had before she became pregnant.

Seventy-two epidemiological studies have been conducted since 1957; and 80% of these studies have shown that abortion increases the risk of breast cancer independently of the effect of delaying the birth of a first child. These epidemiological studies establish a correlation between abortion and increased breast cancer risk. Most of the recent epidemiological studies focus exclusively on the effect of the independent link, not the known risk of delaying the birth of a first child.

> **FAST FACT**
>
> Pregnancy-induced hypertension (high blood pressure) is associated with decreased breast cancer risk.

Support for the Debated Breast Cancer Risk

An independent link is also supported by:

1. Animal research

2. The World Health Organization's acknowledgement that oral contraceptives and hormone replacement therapy containing estrogen and progestin are "Group 1 carcinogens."

3. The established risk showing that a premature birth before 32 weeks gestation more than doubles breast cancer risk. The hormonal changes to the breasts are the same whether the woman has an abortion or a premature birth before 32 weeks gestation.

4. Plausible biological reasons why an abortion leaves a woman more susceptible to breast cancer.

Abortion is an "elective surgical procedure and a woman's exposure to the hormones of early pregnancy—if it is interrupted—is so great, that just one interrupted pregnancy is enough to make a significant difference in her risk."

Because American women already face a high lifetime risk of developing breast cancer of about 12.5 percent, boosting that risk by even a small percentage through the procurement of a single induced abortion is comparable to the risk of lung cancer from long-term heavy smoking. Approximately 1 in 100 women procuring an abortion is expected to die as a result of abortion-induced breast cancer.

Support for the Abortion Link

An authoritative medical text for doctors who specialize in breast diseases—*The Breast: Comprehensive Management of Benign and Malignant Diseases*—discusses the causes of breast cancer. It states that the exposure of the breasts to estrogen for long periods of time proportion-

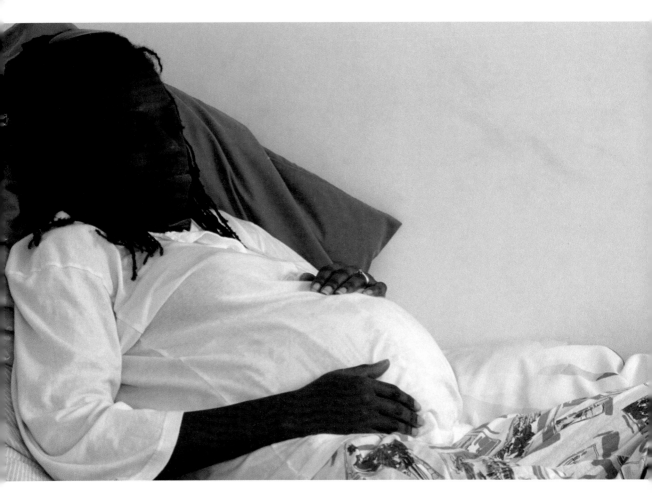

During pregnancy, increased levels of the hormone estrogen cause a woman's breast lobules to multiply. If she has an abortion, there will be more places within her breasts for cancer to start. (Bubbles Photolibrary/Alamy)

ately increases breast cancer risk, and it specifically identifies abortion as a risk factor. It says, "Long-term exposure to endogenous estrogens (early menarche [onset of menstruation]; late menopause; late age at first full-term pregnancy, and being overweight, leading to increased aromatization of circulating androgens to estrogens) appears to increase cancer risk. Risk is decreased only with early menopause (natural or artificial) and childbearing. However, first-trimester abortion increases risk.". . .

The medical text cited the [B.E.] Henderson lecture to support the statement that "first-trimester abortion increases risk." Henderson said, "Recently, we found that a first-trimester abortion, whether spontaneous or induced, before the first full-term pregnancy is actually associated with an increase in the risk of breast cancer."

The Henderson lecture was published in 1988. The statement asserting that abortion is linked with increased breast cancer risk was based on only two studies, the first of which Henderson co-authored and was the first published American study.

Early Evidence of the Abortion Link

Scientists from the National Institutes of Health and the Centers for Disease Control, Bruce Stadel and Phyllis Wingo, and two other prominent epidemiologists were convinced of a link in 1986. They co-authored a letter to the British journal, *Lancet,* and said, "Induced abortion before first term pregnancy increases the risk of breast cancer." They acknowledged the independent effect of an induced abortion on breast cancer risk at a time when there were only two American studies linking abortion with the disease.

Dr. Janet Daling, an abortion supporter, and her colleagues at the Fred Hutchinson Cancer Research Center were commissioned by the National Cancer Institute to conduct a study to determine if induced abortion raises breast cancer risk. The study found that, "among women who had been pregnant at least once, the risk of breast cancer in those who had experienced an induced abortion was 50% higher than among other women."

High Risk Groups

Daling identified 3 high risk groups and reported these findings:

1. Women under the age of 18 or over the age of 29 who obtained induced abortions have more than a twofold increase in risk.

2. Women with a family history of breast cancer who procured an abortion were found to have statistically significant risk increases of 80 percent.

3. Teenagers with a family history of the disease who procured abortions before the age of 18 were found to have incalculably high risk. All 12 women in Daling's study with this background were diagnosed with breast cancer by the age of 45.

An additional high risk group was identified by Dr. Amelia Laing of Howard University:

1. African American women had a 50% increased risk before the age of 40, a 180% increased risk between the ages of 41 and 49 and a 370% increased risk after age 50 if they'd ever procured at least one abortion.

A subsequent study by this author comparing sisters, one of which had procured an abortion, reported a 144% increased risk.

Jane Orient, MD, a spokeswoman for the American Association of Physicians and Surgeons, told World Net Daily that, "If you look at the number of studies that show a connection, they vastly outnumber the ones that don't, and the ones that don't have been criticized for serious methodological flaws." She reported that the elevated risk is "substantial, particularly in women who abort their first pregnancy at a young age and who have a family history of breast cancer. It's something like 800 percent." She added, "I think (doctors) should inform patients about this," and the information "should include the potential connection with breast cancer as well as the long-term psychological risk."

Effects of Delaying a First Full-Term Pregnancy

Medical experts universally agree that it is healthier for a married woman not to postpone her first full-term pregnancy.

One Harvard study reported that each year that a woman postpones her first full-term pregnancy increases her breast cancer risk by 3.5%.

An abortion causes a woman to forego the benefit of increased protection from breast cancer which she would have obtained from an earlier first full-term pregnancy. World Health Organization scientists in 1970 confirmed this saying that, "It is estimated that women having their first child when aged under 18 years have only about one-third the breast cancer risk of those whose first birth is delayed until the age of 35 years or more." In addition, this protective effect was not observed among women who'd had an incomplete first pregnancy.

Childbearing and Breast Cancer

In 2002, the British journal, *Lancet*, published a large meta-analysis by Valerie Beral and her colleagues on the benefits of breastfeeding and childbearing in which data were collected from 47 epidemiological studies in 30 countries. It was found that the relative risk of breast cancer declined 4.3% for each 12 months of breastfeeding and 7.0% for every birth. It was concluded that the incidence of breast cancer in developed nations could be reduced by more than half if only women would bear more children and breastfeed for longer periods of time and that "the lack of or short lifetime duration of breastfeeding typical of women in developed countries makes a major contribution to the high incidence of breast cancer in these countries."

Graham Colditz, MD, a Professor of Medicine at Harvard Medical School and a Professor of Epidemiology at the Harvard Medical School of Public Health, reported that one-half of the differences in the rates of breast cancer between the developed and undeveloped countries are attributable to childbearing patterns, including age at first birth, number of births and breast-feeding. He said, "Comparing the reproductive patterns with six or more pregnancies with the typical pattern of two pregnancies in the developed world, we have shown that at least 50% of the international variation in breast cancer rates can be explained by these patterns of childbearing."

It is known that women, who start their families earlier in their reproductive years, have larger families and breast feed for long periods of time, have a reduced risk of breast cancer. . . .

If American breast cancer rates can be reduced by 50% through a cultural change in childbearing patterns, then it is incumbent on scientists to inform women of these facts and let us make the health decisions for ourselves. The alternative is to continue the status quo at the expense of women's health.

There Is No Relationship Between Abortion and Breast Cancer

National Abortion Federation

The National Abortion Federation [NAF] argues in the following viewpoint that there is no statistical relationship between abortion and an increased risk of breast cancer. The NAF states that many past breast cancer–abortion studies are flawed due to unreliable testing methods. Also covered are some of the issues that have arisen with breast cancer–abortion research. One of the issues discussed is the difference between case-control studies, which are prone to recall bias, and cohort studies, which are not. The National Abortion Federation is a professional medical association based in the United States and Canada. They provide medical, legal, and informational resources.

Breast cancer is a very important health concern for women. For all women, the risk of breast cancer increases with age. According to the National Cancer Institute, this risk rises from about 1 in 252 for a woman in her thirties, to about 1 in 27 for a woman in

SOURCE: "Abortion and Breast Cancer," National Abortion Federation, 2003. Reproduced by permission.

her sixties, to a lifetime risk of about 1 in 8. Discovering the causes of this disease is a high priority for research scientists around the world.

Abortion–Breast Cancer Studies

Since 1981 several dozen studies investigating whether abortion increases a woman's risk of developing breast cancer have been published. The results of the studies often seem contradictory, which can be confusing and frightening for women who are considering having an abortion. Many of the older studies alleging a link between breast cancer and abortion were flawed, since some included only a small number of women, and most used a scientifically unreliable method dependent upon self-reported abortion data. Newer studies that rely on more accurate methods have consistently shown no association between abortion and an increased breast cancer risk.

What the Experts Say

In February 2003, the National Cancer Institute [NCI], a branch of the National Institutes of Health, convened a workshop that evaluated studies on abortion and breast cancer and assessed whether an association between abortion and breast cancer exists. Over 100 of the world's leading experts on pregnancy and breast cancer, including epidemiologists, clinicians and breast cancer advocates participated.

These experts concluded that studies have clearly established that "induced abortion is not associated with an increase in breast cancer risk." This conclusion was reviewed and unanimously approved by the NCI's top scientific advisors and counselors.

Types of Studies

In order to understand which studies give us the most accurate information, it is helpful to know more about how the studies are done. There are two basic ways to conduct

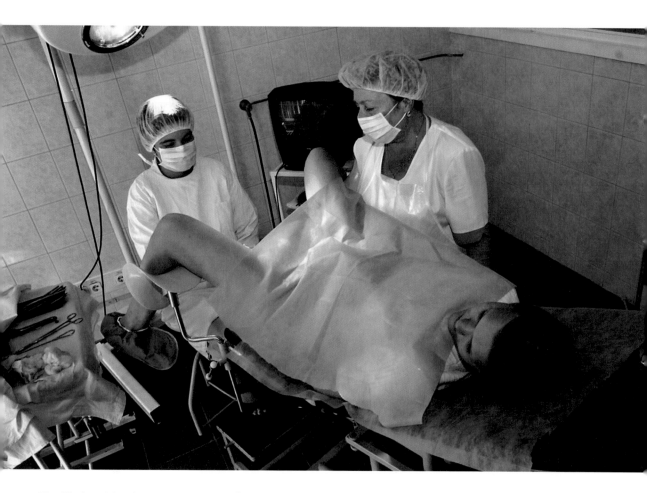

The National Institutes of Health studied abortion and came to the conclusion that the procedure is not associated with an increase in breast cancer risk. **(AP Images)**

research on this topic; one looks backward in time at the abortion experiences of women who have breast cancer, and the other looks forward in time at the development of breast cancer among women who have had abortions.

- In case-control studies, scientists compare women who have breast cancer with similar women who do not. Both groups are asked whether they have had abortions in the past.

- In cohort studies, scientists compare women who have had abortions and similar women who have not. Both groups are examined again as years pass to determine whether they develop breast cancer.

Case-Control Studies and Recall Bias

Of the two, case-control studies have a higher likelihood of inaccurate results because healthy women and women with cancer report information about their medical history differently. When healthy women are asked very personal questions about their sexual lives, especially about a topic as sensitive as abortion, there is a strong tendency not to report truthfully on abortions they have had. On the other hand, women being treated for breast cancer are strongly motivated to give their doctors very accurate information, and they are less likely to forget to report an abortion they have had. Comparing the two groups of women, those with breast cancer will appear to be more likely to have had abortions, even if this is not actually the case. Scientists call this difference in how women report their medical history "recall bias."

A 1996 case-control study among Dutch women demonstrated how recall bias works. Scientists found that in areas of the country where abortion is socially accepted, women with breast cancer and women without breast cancer reported equal numbers of past abortions. But in regions where attitudes about abortion are less tolerant, healthy women reported fewer past abortions than women with breast cancer. Because it is not reasonable to assume that abortion leads to breast cancer in one place but not in another, the researchers concluded that attitudes about abortion led some of the healthy women to under-report their abortions if they lived in places where abortion was not socially accepted. Other case-control studies have found similarly conflicting results, with some suggesting that abortion and breast cancer may be linked, and others finding no connection at all.

> **FAST FACT**
>
> In the largest ever study regarding the abortion–breast cancer link, a Danish study analyzed the abortion histories of 10,246 women among a total of 1,529,512 women studied.

Cohort Studies

Cohort studies are not affected by recall bias, because scientists monitor the women directly from the time of their abortions until the time of any breast cancer diagnosis, and they do not need to rely on potentially faulty memories of past events. Scientists consider the results of cohort studies to be much more accurate than case-control studies. Cohort studies, however, take many years to complete and they are very expensive, so fewer of them are done. Of all cohort studies which have been published to date, none have shown a link between abortion and breast cancer.

The research problems discussed above can be overcome when accurate and complete life-long medical records are kept. In some European countries, where the

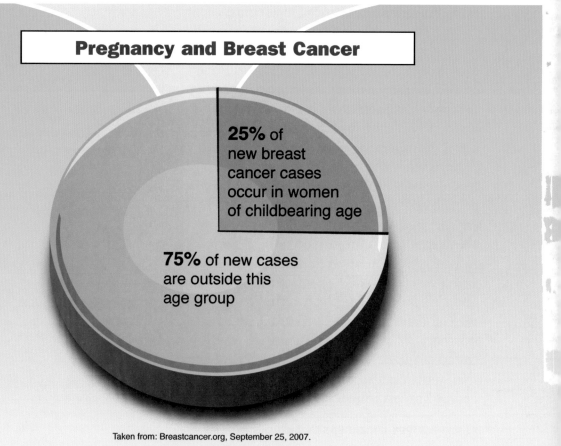

Pregnancy and Breast Cancer

25% of new breast cancer cases occur in women of childbearing age

75% of new cases are outside this age group

Taken from: Breastcancer.org, September 25, 2007.

government maintains a complete health registry on each citizen, studies using these unbiased records can be very informative. In fact, the most convincing cohort study of abortion and breast cancer involved over 1.5 million women in Denmark. Using data from national registries, scientists found that abortion had no overall effect on the risk of breast cancer.

Genetic Screening for Breast Cancer Has Pros and Cons

Breastcancer.org

In the following article a nonprofit breast cancer organization discusses the advantages and disadvantages to genetic screening for breast cancer. One of the advantages is that if a genetic marker is found, an individual can then take preventative measures to help lower her breast cancer risk. A disadvantage is that finding a genetic marker does not mean that an individual will automatically develop breast cancer. According to Breastcancer.org genetic testing can be both a help and a hindrance depending on the individual circumstances. Breastcancer.org is a nonprofit organization providing information about breast cancer.

Anyone wanting to learn the details of her or his genetic makeup should consider both the benefits and drawbacks of knowing such information.

SOURCE: "Seeking Your Genetic Information: Pros and Cons," Breastcancer.org, 2007. Reproduced by permission of Breastcancer. org.

The Pros of Genetic Testing

Here are the advantages of seeking genetic testing if you have a family member with a known breast cancer gene mutation:

If your test result is normal, your genetic counselor can tell you with greater certainty that you have the same relatively low risk of developing breast or ovarian cancer as women in the general population. Routine screening for breast cancer (self-exams, mammograms, doctor visits) will still be important for you, as it is for all women. For ovarian cancer there are currently no widely accepted screening guidelines for women at average risk of developing the disease.

If your test result is abnormal, closely monitoring the health of your breasts and ovaries can help find a cancer in its earliest stage, when it is most treatable and curable.

> **FAST FACT**
>
> Having a BRCA gene mutation raises a woman's lifetime risk of breast cancer to 85 percent.

Possible Courses of Action

If your test result is abnormal:

- You may want to consider taking a medication such as tamoxifen, which could reduce your risk of developing breast cancer. You may also want to participate in a clinical trial on breast cancer prevention to see whether other drugs may be effective.

- You may want to consider preventive (prophylactic) surgical removal of your breasts, ovaries, or both before cancer has an opportunity to form.

- If you do develop cancer, knowing you have a genetic abnormality will give you more information on which to base your treatment decisions.

- If you get genetic testing in a research setting, or if you participate in other clinical studies, you'll be contributing to research that could eventually help to prevent or cure breast or ovarian cancer.

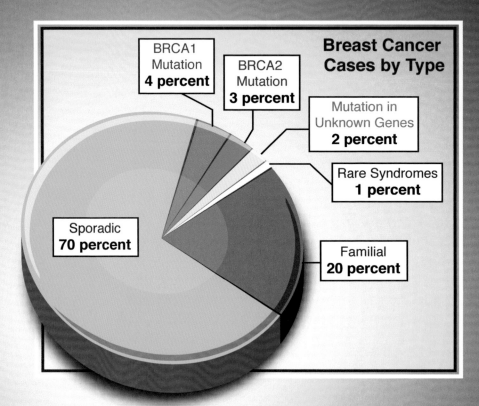

Breast Cancer Cases by Type

BRCA1 Mutation **4 percent**

BRCA2 Mutation **3 percent**

Mutation in Unknown Genes **2 percent**

Rare Syndromes **1 percent**

Sporadic **70 percent**

Familial **20 percent**

Taken from: University of Colorado Cancer Center, 2004. www.uccc.info.

• Finally, knowing that you carry an abnormal breast cancer gene may prompt you and your family members to make lifestyle and family planning changes or decisions to help improve your odds.

The Cons of Genetic Testing

Genetic testing has limitations and possible drawbacks, including:

• It's not yet clear exactly what you should or shouldn't do once you get your genetic test results. We still don't know the most effective ways to prevent breast cancer, although taking tamoxifen could lower your risk of developing the disease.

• Removing the breasts and ovaries to lower cancer risk (called prophylactic surgery) does not get rid of every breast- and ovary-related cell. So even though it can lower your risk a lot, it still does not entirely eliminate the risk. Even after such surgery, a woman with an abnormal breast cancer gene must be monitored regularly. These diseases may show up in nearby tissues and organs.

• Normal test results don't guarantee healthy genes. In some families, many women have had breast cancer, yet they all test normal for the known breast cancer mutations. These families may have an inherited form of breast cancer caused by an abnormality or other gene that simply hasn't been identified yet. A woman from such a family must be followed closely. . . .

• Close monitoring does not always succeed in detecting breast cancer early. Some women end up being diagnosed with later-stage disease despite the best surveillance techniques.

• For some women, an abnormal test result can trigger anxiety, depression, or anger. Even though the result doesn't mean that a woman will definitely get breast cancer, many women with an abnormal gene assume they will. If you think knowing the information may be too hard for you emotionally, consider not having genetic testing until more is known about how to beat the disease.

• If you learn that you've passed on an abnormal gene to your children, you may feel guilty and worried. (Yet such knowledge may also prepare you for helping your children cope with their genetic information.)

• You could face discrimination—in getting insurance coverage or employment—based on your genetic information. Advances in breast cancer genetic testing

A lab technician prepares samples taken from pregnant women for genetic screening. (AGStockUSA, Inc./Alamy)

have outpaced legal protections for those identified through such testing. Although basic legislation exists in the United States to protect most people from such discrimination, privacy remains a serious issue. Carelessness and leaks could reveal your test results to others. So far, however, no cases of discrimination related to genetic information are known to have occurred.

• Genetic testing may not answer all your questions. In families with an abnormal breast cancer gene, other factors that are not yet understood may contribute to high risk.

Genetic Testing Is Most Useful for Only a Small Group of People

Flora Lichtman

Genetic testing kits for breast cancer are becoming more widely available than ever before. In the following selection *Science Friday®* looks at the concerns with these tests and how many women actually benefit from them. Genetic test kit advertisements are not reviewed by any branch of the federal government. This can lead to misplaced concern that an individual may be carrying the breast cancer gene, states the author. These tests cover the BRCA1 and BRCA2 genes, and while mutations in these genes can significantly increase a woman's breast cancer risk, not all mutations to these genes are damaging. The author also states that these tests are only useful for a small number of women with a certain family history.

Flora Lichtman produces content for the *Science Friday®* Web site. *Science Friday®* is a weekly science talk show broadcast on National Public Radio (NPR).

SOURCE: Flora Lichtman, "Genetic Testing for Breast and Ovarian Cancer," *Science Friday®*, September 17, 2007. Reproduced by permission.

P hysicians began peering into our genes over a decade ago to look for mutations that increase the risk of breast and ovarian cancer. Last week [September 2007], Myriad Genetics Inc., a Salt Lake City–based biopharmaceutical company, began mass-marketing this genetic test, called BRACAnalysis, to the general public.

Taking a test that tells you whether you have increased risk of getting cancer might seem like a good thing. But some genetic experts say it may not be, and worry that Myriad' s campaign will prompt people to make important medical decisions based on ad copy, rather than sound medical advice.

No Federal Watchdog

Unlike pharmaceutical ads and labels, which are reviewed by the Food and Drug Administration and the Federal Trade Commission, genetic test advertisements are not subject to any federal oversight, experts say. Concern that the content of the ads may be misleading has prompted an investigation by Connecticut's attorney general.

Mark Robson, a medical oncologist at Memorial Sloan-Kettering Cancer Center (MSKCC) in New York, sums up the concern this way: "I to some extent agree with the premise of the Myriad campaign which is that we're not identifying all those who could potentially benefit from the information. But the great majority of women with breast cancer are not going to carry this pre-disposition." Experts say that of the women diagnosed with breast cancer this year [2007], about 5 percent will have the mutation.

"There's a danger that many people will be concerned they carry the mutation and the flip side is that there may be people who would be falsely reassured when they don't have the predisposition," says Robson, who is also the clinic director of clinical genetics service at MSKCC.

Test Not Publicly Available

Gregory Critchfield, M.D., president of Myriad Genetics, stresses that a consumer cannot order BRACAnalysis directly—a physician must order the test, which should help weed out people who are unlikely to have the mutation. "The BRACAnalysis public awareness campaign is designed to encourage women with breast and ovarian cancer running in their families to talk to their doctors about their risk. The most important part is that conversation with a healthcare professional," Critchfield said

This printout of a BRCA1 gene screening shows variations in the gene that causes a pre-disposition to breast cancer. (Suzanne Long/ Alamy)

```
cttagcggta gccccttggt ttccgtggca acggaaaagc gcgggaatta cagataaatt
aaaactgcga ctgcgcggcg tgagctcgct gagacttcct ggacggggga caggctgtgg
ggtttctcag ataactgggc ccctgcgctc aggaggcctt caccctctgc tctgggtaaa
gttcattgga acagaaagaa atggatttat ctgctcttcg cgttgaagaa gtacaaaatg
tcattaatgc tatgcagaaa atcttagagt gtcccatctg tctggagttg atcaaggaac
ctgtctccac aaagtgtgac cacatatttt gcaaattttg catgctgaaa cttctcaacc
agaagaaagg gccttcacag tgtcctttat gtaagaatga tataaccaaa aggagcctac
aagaaagtac gagatttagt caacttgttg aagagctatt gaaaatcatt tgtgcttttc
agcttgacac aggtttggag tatgcaaaca gctataattt tgcaaaaaag gaaaataact
ctcctgaaca tctaaaagat gaagtttcta tcatccaaag tatgggctac agaaaccgtg
ccaaaagact tctacagagt gaacccgaaa atccttcctt gcaggaaacc agtctcagtg
tccaactctc taaccttgga actgtgagaa ctctgaggac aaagcagcgg atacaacctc
aaaagacgtc tgtctacatt gaattgggat ctgattcttc tgaagatacc gttaataagg
caacttattg cagtgtggga gatcaagaat tgttacaaat cacccctcaa ggaaccaggg
atgaaatcag tttggattct gcaaaaaagg ctgcttgtga attttctgag acggatgtaa
caaatactga acatcatcaa cccagtaata atgatttgaa caccactgag aagcgtgcag
ctgagaggca tccagaaaag tatcagggta gttctgtttc aaacttgcat gtggagccat
gtggcacaaa tactcatgcc agctcattac agcatgagaa cagcagttta ttactcacta
aagacagaat gaatgtagaa aaggctgaat tctgtaataa aagcaaacag cctggcttag
caaggagcca acataacaga tgggctggaa gtaaggaaac atgtaatgat aggcggactc
ccagcacaga aaaaaaggta gatctgaatg ctgatcccct gtgtgagaga aaagaatgga
ataagcagaa actgccatgc tcagagaatc ctagagatac tgaagatgtt ccttggataa
cactaaatag cagcattcag aaagttaatg agtggttttc cagaagtgat gaactgttag
gttctgatga ctcacatgat ggggagtctg aatcaaatgc caaagtagct gatgtattgg
acgttctaaa tgaggtagat gaatattctg gttcttcaga gaaaatagac ttactggcca
gtgatcctca tgaggcttta atatgtaaaa gtgaaagagt tcactccaaa tcagtagaga
gtaatattga agacaaaata tttgggaaaa cctatcggaa gaaggcaagc ctccccaact
taagccatgt aactgaaaat ctaattatag gagcatttgt tactgagcca cagataatac
aagagcgtcc cctcacaaat aaattaaagc gtaaaggag acctacatca ggccttcatc
ctgaggattt tatcaagaaa gcagatttgg cagttcaaaa gactcctgaa atgataaatc
agggaactaa ccaaacggag cagaatggtc aagtgatgaa tattactaat agtggtcatg
agaataaaac aaaaggtgat tctattcaga atgagaaaaa tcctaaccca atagaatcac
```

in an interview. Myriad's position is that only a small percentage of people with an inherited risk factor know about it and this campaign will likely encourage more people to take the test to find out.

BRACAnalysis, which costs about $3000 for the full analysis, looks for variations in the DNA of two genes—BRCA1 and BRCA2. The BRCA1 and BRCA2 sequences are the blueprints for proteins that protect against breast and ovarian cancers. By reading the sequences of the parts of the genes that code for the protein, Myriad can identify potentially harmful variations in the genes.

Gene Mutations and Variations

Certain variations, called deleterious mutations, in BRCA1 and BRCA2 can prevent the genes from making functioning proteins. These mutations significantly increase the risk of getting breast or ovarian cancer: A woman with a deleterious variation has a 56 to 87 percent risk of developing breast cancer by age 70, compared with a 7 percent risk in the general population. For ovarian cancer, the risk of getting the disease is 2 percent in the general population, while women with the mutation have a 27 to 44 percent risk, according to Myriad.

Not all variations in these two genes, however, are necessarily harmful. "There's over 1000 different variants that have been described already in each of these genes," says Lawrence Brody, a senior investigator at the National Human Genome Research Institute. Some of these variations (the deleterious ones) are known to increase cancer risk, others are known to not increase risk, and a third category of variations are not well-understood.

This category, "variants of uncertain significance," are the results that physicians and geneticists would be hard-pressed to usefully interpret. "Typically many of us view the middle ground as essentially uninformative. If we see that kind of report we say, 'OK, we're not at a point of knowing what that means, let's go back to your family

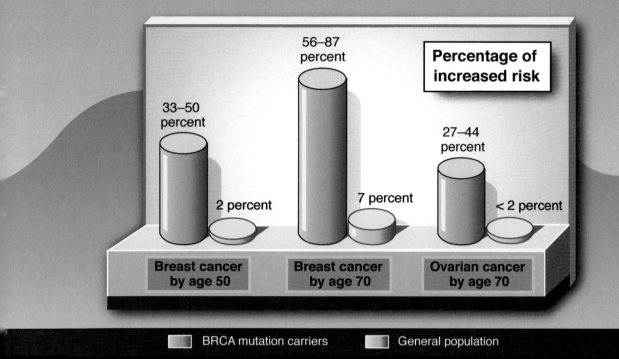

BRCA Mutation Increases the Risk of Cancer

56–87 percent

Percentage of increased risk

33–50 percent

27–44 percent

2 percent

7 percent

< 2 percent

Breast cancer by age 50

Breast cancer by age 70

Ovarian cancer by age 70

BRCA mutation carriers

General population

Taken from: Jacob International, 2008. www.jacobintl.org.

history,'" says Sharon Plon, professor in the departments of pediatrics and human genetics and the director of the medical scientist training program at Baylor College of Medicine in Houston, Texas.

Even if a patient's test results unambiguously point to higher cancer risk, what she should then do may not always be obvious. The options are limited: the patient can increase surveillance for breast cancer (by getting full body MRIs instead of mammograms), or decide to get her breasts or ovaries removed.

Who Benefits?

Sharon Plon—who advises patients on whether to get genetic tests like this one—says that the test is most useful for people with a specific family history. Good candidates for the test are women who have had close relatives (mothers and sisters) with early-onset breast cancer, women with ovarian cancer in their family, families in which multiple family members have had breast cancer, and women who have had multiple instances of breast cancer. In fact, the best candidates for the test are those already diagnosed with breast or ovarian cancer, Plon says. If they are found to have a deleterious variation, their relatives can then be tested for that specific variation—a cheaper and less-involved analysis.

As the cost of genome sequencing goes down, it's feasible that more genetic tests that look for genes with less significant risks may be marketed. But do people want to know such hazy predictions? As for the BRCA1 BRCA2 test, the president of Myriad says business is booming. "The number of tests every year continues to grow every year very strongly. This is becoming something people know a lot about and are expressing a lot of interest in," says Critchfield.

Brody is less certain. "Information seeking does seem to be a natural tendency," Brody says, "but if it doesn't help you in any way . . . it's unlikely that it will become widespread." A look at the results of Myriad's campaign may be the best indication of whether or not people really do want to know their genetic horoscopes.

FAST FACT

For a woman testing positive for the BRCA1 or BRCA2 gene, there is a 50 percent chance that her child will also test positive.

Breast Cancer Screening Is Not Always Necessary

Breast Cancer Action

In the following article the Breast Cancer Action group discusses why mammography screening may not always be in an individual's best health interests. In recent years there has been a growing debate about whether or not mammography is a necessary and reliable screening tool. One of the main arguments the author puts forth is that early detection does not always equal a cure in the case of breast cancer. Also discussed is the accuracy and effectiveness of several different screening methods. Breast Cancer Action is an advocacy organization focusing on eliminating breast cancer and providing information on breast cancer issues.

Since the early 1980s, the United States' public campaign to eradicate breast cancer has focused largely on efforts that promote mammography screening. Since the early 1900s, Breast Cancer Action (BCA) has raised concerns about the effectiveness of mammography screening, and the dangers of misleading the public about

SOURCE: "Policy on Breast Cancer Screening and 'Early Detection,'" Breast Cancer Action, October 2006. Reproduced by permission.

the benefits of "breast cancer early detection." Throughout our history, BCA has encouraged women to make informed decisions for themselves about whether to take advantage of the technology.

Mammography Debate

In recent years, mammography screening—mammograms given to healthy women with no symptoms of any breast problem—has been the subject of considerable debate within the medical community, particularly with respect to its use among premenopausal women, and, increasingly, with respect to its effectiveness as a screening tool for women of any age. BCA believes that the widespread use of mammog-

A woman has her breast screened on a mammography machine. Critics question the value of mammography screening. (Picture Partners/Alamy)

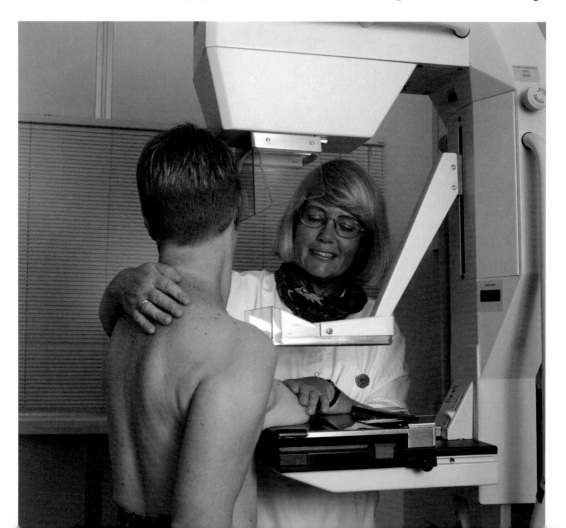

raphy and the controversy over its uses dictate that women of all ages be fully informed about the risks and benefits of mammograms.

BCA also believes that once women are fully informed about mammograms, each woman [should] make her own decision about whether or not to make use of the technology. Informed consent, in this case, presents women with difficult choices. Those who choose to have screening mammograms should have ready access to the best available technology, with the expense covered by their health insurance or the government.

> **FAST FACT**
>
> In controlled studies, mammography has been shown to reduce the probability of dying from breast cancer an average of 16 percent.

Early Detection Does Not Equal a Cure

Many breast cancer awareness and education campaigns are focused on the idea that "early detection is your best protection." They also carry the assurance that "breast cancer found early is almost 100 percent curable." But the promotion of mammography screening actually masks the real issue in breast cancer diagnosis: the value of "early" detection. While 98 percent of women diagnosed at a localized stage are alive five years after diagnosis, this does not mean that these women have been cured of breast cancer.

Being cancer-free for five years following diagnosis is accurately considered a cure for some cancers. But breast cancer is an exception: it can and does recur at any time, though the likelihood of recurrence is highest in the first two years following treatment, and declines over time.

The Three Groups of Breast Cancer

Many breast cancer awareness campaigns urging women to have yearly mammograms are based on the premise that breast cancer found early can always be effectively treated. But the complex biology of breast cancer means that women diagnosed with "early" breast cancer fall into one of three groups.

- One group has a very aggressive disease that, no matter how small it is when it is found, cannot be effectively treated with the therapies that are currently available. These women will die of breast cancer eventually, no matter what treatment they are given, unless they die of something else first.
- Another group of women diagnosed with breast cancer has a type of either non-aggressive invasive disease or some presentations of DCIS (ductal carcinoma in situ) that will never be life-threatening.
- The third group has a type of breast cancer that responds to currently available treatments. Finding breast cancer earlier does increase the likelihood that treatment will work for women in this group.

We do not know how many women historically have fallen into each of these three groups. And, while these divisions and the treatments currently available mean that "early detection" only matters for women in the third group, we cannot determine at the time of diagnosis the type of tumor a woman has. The result is that we mistreat or over-treat many women diagnosed with breast cancer.

The Main Screening Methods

It is in this framework that we need to examine the three methods of screening that are currently used or recommended for breast cancer detection in the United States: mammography, breast self-exam (BSE), and clinical breast exam (CBE). Thermography—the use of heat sensors to detect breast changes—has not been thoroughly evaluated as a breast cancer screening technology, and is therefore not generally accepted in this country as a screening method.

Mammograms use low-dose X-rays to examine the breast. (X-rays are ionizing radiation, a known carcinogen which has a cumulative effect on the body. The greater the radiation exposure/dose over a lifetime, the greater the risk of radiation-induced cancer. This risk is highest in tissue in which cells are rapidly changing, such as the breast tissue of adolescent females.)

Breast self exams involve women using their own hands and visual inspection on a regular basis to look for changes in their breasts.

Clinical breast exams are also a manual exam, done by health care professionals who periodically examine a woman's breasts for any palpable masses.

Annual clinical breast exams by trained health professionals and breast self exams are essential aspects of breast cancer screening, and should begin with a woman's first gynecological exam or no later than at age 20. While there is controversy over whether BSE saves lives, there is clear evidence that women who do monthly breast self exams detect many breast changes. BCA encourages women to know their own bodies and to see a medical provider if they find any changes in their breasts.

Screening Accuracy

Because mammograms are the only technology medically accepted for breast cancer screening, and because the federal government and many cancer charities promote their use for breast cancer screening, they are in widespread use. But mammograms, BSE and CBE do not always detect breast cancer and are not always accurate. Mammograms, self-exams and clinical breast exams do not always detect breast cancer—causing "false negative" results (when a detection method fails to find a breast cancer that is present). In day-to-day practice, mammograms can miss more than a quarter of all tumors.

All screening methods also result in "false positive" findings, leading to unnecessary biopsies with increased stress and anxiety, as well as physical scarring. One-third

Mammography Screening by Age Group

Percentage of women who received a mammogram
in the past two years, by age group, 1987–2003

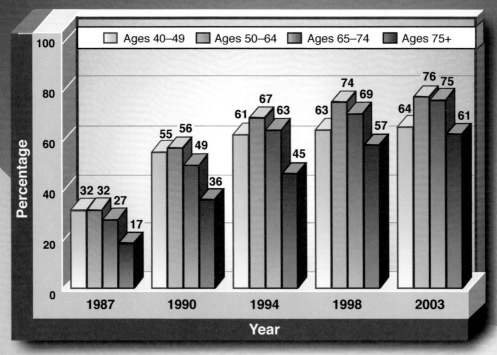

Taken from: National Health Interview Survey (National Center for Health Statistics 2005).
Source: McCarthy and Leatherman, Performance Snapshots, 2006. www.cmwf.org/snapshots.

of women screened over a decade will experience at least one false-positive mammogram result.

Resources should be focused on training health care providers in effective clinical breast exam techniques, developing better treatments for the kinds of breast cancer that we are currently unable to treat effectively, and developing techniques for distinguishing those who can be helped by treatments from those who either don't need treatment or cannot currently be effectively treated.

Low-Fat Diet May Help Breast Cancer

Charlene Laino

In the following selection from a leading medical information Web site, Charlene Laino reports that a recent study has shown that a low-fat diet can make a difference in the recurrence of breast cancer. Over two thousand women were studied, with almost one thousand following a thorough nutrition program. The main intention of the program was to reduce daily fat intake to less than 20 percent of an individual's daily calories. As Laino explains, the women following the nutritional program saw a marked reduction in their risk of cancer recurrence. She also explains that the researchers conducting the study are not certain exactly what program factors were responsible for the risk reduction. Laino is a writer, editor, and contributor to health publications worldwide.

Updated results from what researchers call the first study to directly show that lifestyle changes can improve the outlook for people with cancer suggests a low-fat diet can help prevent breast cancer recurrence.

SOURCE: Charlene Laino, "Low-Fat Diet May Help Breast Cancer," *WebMD*, December 16, 2006. Reproduced by permission.

In the study of more than 2,400 postmenopausal women with early breast cancer, those who cut down on fats in their diet were about one-fifth less likely to either suffer a recurrence or die over the next six to seven years, compared with those who continued to eat their usual foods, according to the updated report.

Women whose tumors were not fueled by hormones—about 30% of women with breast cancer—benefited most. Their chance of recurrence was cut by more than half, and their risk of dying was slashed by two-thirds, says researcher Rowan T. Chlebowski, MD, a medical oncologist at the Los Angeles Biomedical Institute at the Harbor-University of California–Los Angeles Medical Center in Torrance, Calif.

"That's as good or better than any treatment intervention we have for this type of disease," which is notoriously difficult to treat, says C. Kent Osborne, MD, a breast cancer specialist at Baylor College of Medicine in Houston who was not involved with the work.

In contrast, there was little benefit for women with hormone-receptor-positive tumors. The growth of those breast cancers is fueled by hormones; it's the most common type of the disease.

> **FAST FACT**
>
> A woman who has more than two drinks containing alcohol per day increases her risk of invasive breast cancer by 43 percent. Women who average not quite one drink a day increase their risk by 9 percent.

Low-Fat Diet and Breast Cancer

The study, presented . . . at the San Antonio Breast Cancer Symposium, included 2,437 women aged 48 to 75. All had surgery to remove breast tumors, followed by radiation, chemotherapy, and hormone treatment, if needed. Every three months, they all got general dietary guidance.

But nearly 1,000 of the women also entered an intensive nutrition program, which included eight one-on-one sessions with a dietitian every other week, followed by quarterly visits. There were also monthly support groups.

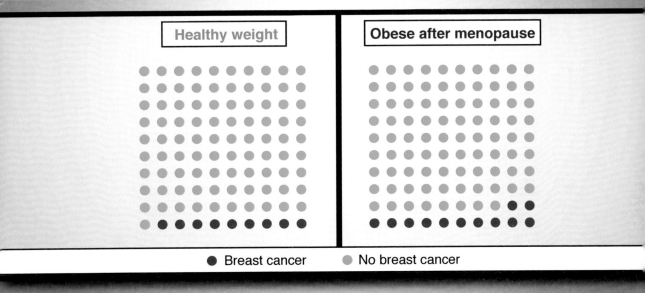

Obesity and Breast Cancer

Of 100 women of healthy weight, 9 develop breast cancer. Of 100 women with obesity after menopause, 12 will develop breast cancer.

Healthy weight

Obese after menopause

● Breast cancer   ● No breast cancer

Taken from: Breakthrough Breast Cancer, 2006. www.breakthrough.org.uk.

The dietitian asked patients what they were eating and taught them which foods contained fat and how much fat—even how to count fat grams. The goal was to reduce dietary fat intake to 20% or less of daily calories, compared with 45% for the average American.

Breast Cancer Risk Cut

The women who received intensive counseling reduced the amount of fat in their diet from 57 grams per day to about 38 grams a day, or from 29% to 19% of their total daily calories.

They were rewarded with a modest amount of weight loss—shedding about six pounds more than those who continued to eat their typical foods.

By nearly six years later, cancer had recurred in about 11% of those on the low-fat diet, compared with more than 13% of those on their usual diet. That translates to about a 21% relative reduction in risk, Chlebowski says.

Put another way, if 36 women adopted the low-fat diet, there would be one fewer nonfatal relapse, he tells WebMD.

In addition, 10% of the women on the usual diet died, vs. 8% of those on the low-fat plan—translating to a 22% reduction in risk.

Among the subgroup of women whose cancers were not fueled by hormones, only 6% who counted fat grams died, compared with 17% who followed their usual diet.

For the updated analysis, researchers at all 39 centers participating in the study provided six-year data; 10 centers also offered seven-year data.

What Should a Woman Do?

Researchers say it's too soon to conclude that counting fat grams is the latest weapon in the war on cancer. But skipping the cheese and crackers won't hurt—and might help.

"This is a seminal study that suggests that following a low-fat diet may help prevent relapses, particularly among women with hormone-receptor-negative disease," says Richard Elledge, MD, a breast cancer specialist at Baylor College of Medicine in Houston and co-moderator of the session.

But, Elledge says, breast cancer survivors who have trouble sticking to a low-fat diet should not feel guilty. "This is just one study," he tells WebMD.

Kay Blanchard, MD, a breast surgeon at Baylor College of Medicine in Houston, says reducing fats "has obvious heart health benefits. In terms of breast cancer, it may even provide additional benefit," she tells WebMD.

Making the changes is "all about substitution and reduction," Chlebowski says.

Breakfast should be cereal and low-fat milk instead of sweet rolls or baked goods. Snack on popcorn—not cheese and crackers. Skip the spread on the bread, the salad dressing on the salad. You can still eat meat; just cut down on portion size, he says.

Regular visits with a nutritionist are critical to sticking with the plan long-term, he adds.

Proponents of low-fat dieting say that such diets can reduce the chance of cancer recurring by one-fifth. **(Nick Gregory/Alamy)**

More Study Needed

Everyone agrees more study is needed. For example, researchers can't say with certainty whether it was the low-fat diet, the weight loss, or maybe some other factor —like an increase in fiber-rich fruits and vegetables— that should get the credit for the women's better health.

They also don't know why women with hormone-receptor-negative cancer benefited so much and those with hormone-positive cancer benefited so little.

Chlebowski says he and the team he works with plan to look at whether a low-fat diet, combined with weight loss and exercise, can prevent cancer comebacks in women with hormone-receptor-negative cancer. That study should kick off next year [2007].

Diet Does Not Lessen Breast Cancer Recurrence

Associated Press

In the following article the Associated Press reports that diet may not have as much to do with breast cancer recurrence as previously thought. A recently completed study found that even though two groups of women had very different diets, both groups experienced almost the same rate of breast cancer recurrence. The mortality rate for both groups was also similar. During the study all women kept a food journal, and the study authors found that while the women accurately reported how many fruits and vegetables were being consumed, they did not report as accurately the total amount of calories being taken in daily. The Associated Press is a news organization providing print, photos, graphics, audio, and video.

Hopes that a diet low in fat and chock-full of fruits and vegetables could prevent the return of breast cancer were dashed [in 2007] by a large, seven-year experiment in more than 3,000 women. The

SOURCE: Associated Press, "Dietary Hopes Dashed for Breast Cancer Patients," msnbc.msn.com, August 31, 2007. Reprinted with permission of the Associated Press.

[U.S.] government study found no benefit from a mega-veggies-and-fruit diet over the U.S. recommended servings of five fruits and vegetables a day—more than most Americans get.

No Weight Lost

Researchers noted that none of the breast cancer survivors lost weight on either diet. That led some experts to suggest that weight loss and exercise should be the next frontier for cancer prevention research. The study appears in the *Journal of the American Medical Association*. "It sends us back to the drawing board," said Susan Gapstur of Northwestern University's Feinberg School of Medicine, who wasn't involved in the new study but co-wrote an accompanying editorial in the journal.

"Should we really have focused on dietary components like fruits, vegetables and fat?" Gapstur asked. "Or should we be focusing, in addition to diet, on lifestyle factors including physical activity and weight?"

For now, the message for the 2.4 million breast cancer survivors in the United States is that they don't need to go overboard on veggies, researchers said.

"This should really lift some of the guilt if women are feeling, 'I'm just not doing enough,'" said study co-author Marcia Stefanick of Stanford University.

The research was kicked off by a $5 million grant from the late Wal-Mart heir John Walton and got an additional $30 million in support from the National Cancer Institute.

Beyond "Folklore"

Walton wanted to support a scientific study so cancer survivors wouldn't have to "rely on folklore," said John Pierce, head of cancer prevention at the University of California, San Diego, who led the research.

Earlier research on whether a healthy diet prevents breast cancer has shown mixed results. The new study

A government study of three thousand women found no benefit in a low-fat diet of fruits and vegetables in fighting breast cancer. (Davis Wilkinson/Alamy)

was designed to be more rigorous. In this experiment, all the women had been successfully treated for early stage breast cancer. Their average age was 53 when the study began.

A Diet Comparison

A group of 1,537 women were randomly assigned to a daily diet that included five vegetable servings, three fruit servings, 16 ounces of vegetable juice and 30 grams of fiber. In most cases, a serving equaled a half-cup. French fries and iceberg lettuce couldn't be counted as vegetables.

The women were allowed to eat meat, but were told to get no more than 15 percent to 20 percent of their calories from fat, a goal they ultimately were unable to achieve. "That's a tough diet," said Pierce, who ate that way himself along with his staff and the women in the study.

As a comparison, another 1,551 women were assigned to get educational materials about the importance of eating five servings of fruits and vegetables a day.

The women in both groups kept food diaries regularly, but not daily, through the course of the study.

During the next seven years, the cancer returned in about the same proportion of women in both groups: 256 women (16.7 percent) of the women on the special diet and 262 women (16.9 percent) in the comparison group. About 10 percent of both groups died during that time, most of them from breast cancer.

Calorie Conflict

It didn't matter whether the breast cancer was the most common type—fueled by hormones—or not; the special diet didn't prevent the cancer from coming back. Those results run counter to a previous study by different researchers that suggested low-fat diets may help prevent the return of the type of breast cancer that is not linked to hormones.

In the mega-veggies group, the women changed their eating habits substantially, mostly by increasing fruits and vegetables to as much as 11 servings a day. They failed to meet the fat target, but did eat 13 percent less in fat calories than did the comparison group.

After one year, women on the high-vegetable diet had 73 percent higher blood levels of carotenoids (pigments found in fruits and vegetables) than the other women.

> **FAST FACT**
>
> An Iowa Women's Health Study reports that women who eat their red meat cooked well-done have an almost five times higher risk of breast cancer.

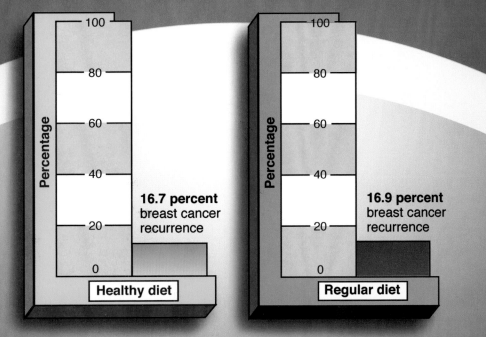

Effect of Diet on Breast Cancer Recurrence

In a randomized trial discussed in the *Journal of the American Medical Association*, a higher-fiber, lower-fat, healthier diet had no effect on breast cancer recurrence.

16.7 percent breast cancer recurrence

Healthy diet

16.9 percent breast cancer recurrence

Regular diet

Taken from: J.P. Pierce, "Women's Healthy Eating and Living Well Randomized Trial," *Journal of the American Medical Association*, July 18, 2007.

That indicates they were truthful about how many fruits and vegetables they ate, Pierce said.

But they may not have been so honest about the calories they ate. The super-veggie group gained 1.3 pounds and the comparison group gained 0.88 pound, on average. "There's no question they were underreporting on calories, especially the heavier women," Pierce said, or they would have lost weight.

The Courage of
Breast Cancer Patients

Jennie Nash

Jennie Nash is the author of The Victoria's Secret Catalog Never Stops Coming and Other Lessons I Learned from Breast Cancer. *In the following selection Nash tells how she felt about her scheduled lumpectomy and the damage it would inflict on her. She also describes the occasion of wearing a red gown to a formal black and white ball because a black dress just did not feel correct to her given her recent breast cancer diagnosis. Unbeknownst to her, Nash was the source of courage for many people there for not letting her cancer get in the way of anything.*

Two weeks after I was diagnosed with breast cancer, there was a silent auction at our church. I'd been on the committee that was putting the party together, and I knew what a great event it was going to be: great music, great food, and a room full of people feeling

Photo on facing page. It is important that breast cancer victims get support from friends and family in battling the disease. (Michael Dwyer/Alamy)

SOURCE: Jennie Nash, *Chicken Soup for the Breast Cancer Survivor's Soul: Stories to Inspire, Support and Heal.* Deerfield Beach, FL: Health Communications, 2006. Copyright © 2006 Jack Canfield, Mark Victor Hansen. All rights reserved. Reproduced by permission.

festive and spending money for a good cause. Our theme was "Black and White, Starry Night" and, like the famed Black and White Ball, everyone would wear either black or white. For months, while working on the invitations and soliciting donations, I'd envisioned myself wearing my favorite black-tie outfit. My husband loved it, and I always felt grown-up when I wore it—wise and worldly and sexy—and it was black as night.

But I was scheduled to have a lumpectomy five days after the event—a procedure where a breast surgeon takes a slice of tissue from your breast, as if from an orange or an apple pie—and somehow a black dress didn't feel right. I realized this would be the last public and formal event I'd ever attend with both breasts still intact.

This diagram shows a lumpectomy procedure for removing cancerous tumors from a breast. (**Nucleus Medical Art, Inc./Alamy**)

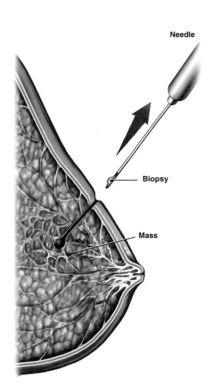

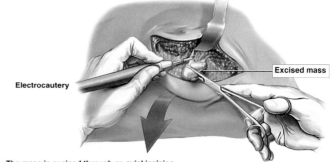

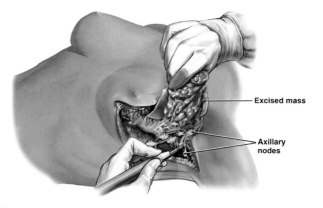

A. A fine needle biopsy is performed on the suspicious mass.

B. The mass is excised through an axial incision.

C. The breast tissue surrounding the initial lumpectomy and the axillary lymph nodes are excised.

Breast Function

I have, over the years, grown rather attached to my breasts. When I was in high school and college, I didn't think much about them—they were average B-cup breasts, so what was there to think? They didn't bounce too much when I played tennis, they filled out any dress or shirt I chose to wear, became marginally tender once a month, and were two of the primary reasons my boyfriend was able to say he liked my curves.

The process of pregnancy, breastfeeding and motherhood, however, gave my breasts a whole new level of value. It made them, for one thing, a cup size bigger. They were plump and full, which made that same boyfriend—now my husband—pay even more attention, which was flattering and fun. Making babies also made my breasts functional. I breastfed both children for nine months each and was proud I could produce all those antibodies, all that concentrated protein.

I was three years past breastfeeding when cancer was diagnosed, and down a breast size from finally losing the weight of childbearing, so my breasts were, in some ways, past their prime. I didn't need them to please a man because Rob now knew there was far more to me than just my curves. For all practical intents and purposes, I didn't need my breasts to go on living a happy and healthy life, but the lumpectomy was still going to do them damage—and damage to your own flesh isn't something you can just offhandedly accept.

A Dress Never Worn

The night of the party started out at a frantic pace—I was left with just ten minutes to get dressed. I ran into the house, went to pull out the dress and stopped. Hanging next to the black velvet was a long, luxurious raspberry-red gown with a deep V-neck in front and a deeper V in back. I'd never worn it.

I bought the dress with my sister, for no good reason, on sale at a little boutique. I had put on the Nicole Miller gown just for fun, stepped out of the dressing room to preen in front of the mirror and was met with the stares of every woman in the shop.

"That dress was made for you," one woman said.

"You're buying it," my sister declared.

The dress was perfect—a simple forties movie-star dress that was curvy in exactly the same places I was. I had absolutely nowhere to wear such a dress, but bought it and stuck it in the back of my closet for two years.

I made a split-second decision: I was going to wear the red dress. Because of its deep Vs, I couldn't wear a regular bra, but I thought, Why wear one?

I slipped the dress over my bare body and felt the cool glide of the satin lining fall from my shoulders to my ankles. I felt the fabric brush against my breasts. I pinned up my hair, put on some bright red lipstick and took off—to be the only woman wearing a colored dress in a room full of black and white.

A Confident Woman

I've never been a woman who turned heads. I have never felt confident enough in my looks to carry myself in such a way that I would. That night, however, I felt like the most beautiful woman in the world. I felt wholly alive in that red dress, and people must have picked up on the electricity, as if it were a fragrance. Men and women alike, people I knew and people I didn't know, came up to me to tell me how spectacular I looked, what a gorgeous dress I had on.

"You seem to glow," they said, and I loved the feeling of swishing around the room, feeling the weight of that dress as it draped to the floor, feeling it cool and clean on my bare breasts, which for that one last night, anyway, were still mine.

Many in that room were aware of my diagnosis and fear. The Sunday before, every hymn we sang in church made me cry, so I'd had to walk out of the service every ten minutes. But not one of my fellow parishioners mentioned my diagnosis the night of the party. It wasn't as if they were afraid or being sensitive or polite. It was as if my wearing the red dress prohibited the very idea of breast cancer, like a shield of armor.

A Source of Courage

A few days later, I got a call from the head of the party committee, thanking me for my help—which I'd abruptly stopped giving two weeks before. "We finally got everything cleaned up," she said, "and you were the hottest topic of discussion around the dish-drying rack."

"Me?" I said, thinking of the way church ladies chatter and gossip, and wondering what I could possibly have done.

"You were the most beautiful woman in the room that night, Jennie, and the most courageous. A lot of women in your shoes wouldn't have even shown up, let alone worn that dress."

Courageous? I thought. Courageous? So that was what courage felt like—that rush of judgment to know just what to do—or wear—that sense of satisfaction that nothing—not even cancer—was going to stand in the way of feeling utterly confident, that sweet perfume of feeling completely and totally alive. If that was courage, it suited me as well as the red dress.

I'd like to frame it.

A Man Recounts His Mastectomy

William C. Rands III

William C. Rands III is a Detroit-based businessman and philanthropist. In the following selection he explains what it was like to be a man and diagnosed with breast cancer. Rands describes in detail the physical and emotional processing he went through while being treated for his cancer. Especially important to him is the support of other cancer patients and survivors and the help and advice they can provide. Another factor that Rands discusses is deciding the best course of action to take in the face of massive amounts of medical information. He explains how, with the help of his wife, Happy, he moved from cancer patient to cancer survivor.

I consider myself incredibly fortunate. Like most men, I don't even know that I could get breast cancer. But it developed in a place where it could be removed, I was lucky enough to find it early, and I had great medical

SOURCE: S. David Nathanson, *Ordinary Miracles.* Westport, CT: Praeger Publishers, 2007. Copyright © 2007 by S. David Nathanson, M.D. All rights reserved. Reproduced by permission of Greenwood Publishing Group, Inc., Westport, CT.

care and support. I would not trade what I have learned and experienced in this journey for anything, and in that sense I would have to say it has enriched my life more than it has impoverished it. In deference to the many, many people whose journey is much tougher than mine, I must state that I would not utter that previous sentence if I did not feel I could consider myself a survivor. I have lived to go on to other things and to do my tiny bit to help others and to fight the tragic and burdensome disease of breast cancer.

Advice for the Journey

If I could offer two pieces of advice to anyone who finds herself, or importantly himself, on such a journey, these would be the following. First, there are times when you will just go along with what the doctors say, because there is no logical choice. But there are also times when there are real choices and if you are ready to take control of your care when the time is right, it will help you a lot, both physically and emotionally. Second, we cancer patients and survivors really stick together. The support and advice I received from fellow patients (of course mostly women) has been overwhelming and absolutely vital to my outcome. A consequence of this thought is that we each have a duty to help others when we can. What seems like a piece of mundane factual information from someone who has been

> **FAST FACT**
>
> Male breast cancer strikes most often between the ages of sixty and seventy.

through it can be a wondrous lifting of the fear of the unknown. I have felt comfortable being completely open and communicative about what I have experienced. Actually, when I started writing this, I worried that it would be a bad experience to relive a part of my life that was really difficult at the time. But it has been very positive for me, and I hope the result is not too colored by the happy outcome to be useful to the reader. . . .

Finding the Cancer

I discovered it in the shower. I couldn't figure out why a spot right next to my right nipple seemed hard and somewhat sore. It was August 1999, at our summer cottage, which is on Lake Huron and not near to my doctor's office. I didn't know what it was, but I knew it was something I didn't understand and didn't like. I was about due for an annual physical, and so a week later when we were

A surgeon performs a needle biopsy on a woman's breast. Biopsies are used to reveal cancerous tumors. (Beranger/ Curie/Photo Researchers, Inc.)

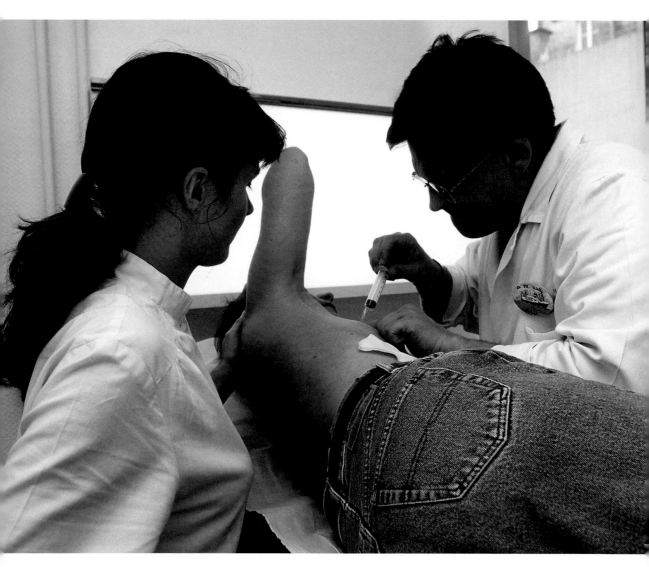

home I made an appointment. I loved my doctor, a guy who would talk to me as an intellectual colleague and not a patient to be ordered around. Sadly, soon after that, he died of kidney cancer himself. We had jousted a bit about whether I would accept the idea of taking a blood pressure medicine. He never talked down to me; he just presented me with the medical evidence. Also he had said I would benefit from losing a few pounds.

I remember the physical examination very well. I actually had it in my mind to notice whether he would find the lump, and he did not. But when he was finished he said, "Now, is there anything else you would like to talk about?"

I said, "Here, check this out."

He felt the lump and said, "Well, I see about three of these a year in men, but I have yet to find the elusive male breast cancer. However, I definitely want to get this biopsied."

He made an appointment for me with the plastic surgeon in the same clinic, and about a week later I was in his office. It seemed a little weird that he took a picture of my chest before he started the biopsy, so I absorbed myself in admiring the closeup lens on the camera because it had little light sources right around the lens. He numbed the area but I remember that when he went back for some more tissue he went beyond the margin of the anesthetic. Ouch! He made some comment about the biopsy not leaving much of a scar but if it turned out to be cancer it would require some "disfiguring surgery." I recall that remark not being very reassuring at the time, but I rested my emotions on my doctor's comment that he did not expect it to be anything significant. I had to wait a week for the results.

One week later was the morning of my fifty-sixth birthday. It was 8 o'clock in the morning and I was sitting on the plastic surgeon's examining table with my legs hanging over the side. He approached me with a piece of paper, and said, "The report is positive for carcinoma." All the blood went out of my head. I really had to hold on to the table to keep from falling off. The doctor gave me the one-page pathology report and I read: "Carcinoma of the breast, poorly differentiated, grade 3." I remember asking him what the grade meant and he said that the cancer was aggressive. After I composed myself and was told I would have an appointment made for me with a doctor named N., I took the one-page report to my own doctor's office in the Internal Medicine Department.

I asked them to make a copy of it for me and to give me an envelope. I wrote on the report, "Gary, you found it this time," and left it for my doctor. I went home to tell my wife and we cried together. We called our daughter in New York and she cried with us. We called our son in Colorado, who was quiet and stunned. Later that evening my doctor called me at home. He said, "Bill, what happened?"

"Well, you told me you wanted me to lose a few pounds."

"Yes," he said, "but not this way!"

I said something about the blood pressure medicine, and he said, "Let's not worry about that right now."

Doctor N. is an impressively neat and efficient man with a kind, calming disposition and what I thought at first was an Australian accent but which I later learned is South African. I could tell he was a special doctor by the relationship he had with his staff, especially the nurses. After examining me briefly and looking at the pathology report, he rolled his chair toward me and said, "You need a mastectomy."...

Always Take Notes

During my first two visits with Dr. N. I learned something that now seems quite obvious to me: when I am in a doctor's office and being told something that will change my life forever I lose track of all the questions I was going to ask, and when I come out I can't really remember what happened. So I have taken to writing notes on a little piece of paper. I think I remember most of what went on during the first visit, but I know that during my second appointment, when he was explaining that there was about a 30 percent chance of lymph node involvement, I mostly went blank. When I got home all I knew was that I had to go in for surgery and that the surgery itself would reveal more bad or good news that I would have to deal with.

Shortly after that visit when there was less than a week to go before the surgery, a most important thing happened. I began to learn how important we cancer patients/survivors are to each other. I was talking on the phone with an old friend who had just finished her chemo and radiation, and she said, "You must ask about Sentinel Node Biopsy. I didn't have it but I wish I had." This simple statement started me on a path of learning and questioning. I learned that Sentinel Lymph Node Biopsy, or SLNB, was an ancillary surgical procedure aimed at avoiding the removal of 25 or so lymph nodes around the underarm and breast area, which had a complication rate of 50–60 percent. The complications are ugly: weakness, pain, swelling of the arm, loss of motion, all of which would have impacted me greatly because I lead an active life. . . .

This was the first of several times when I had to prepare myself to make a decision. Off to the Internet I went and found one of the original studies on SLNB, headed by a Dr. Krag. The article stated that the procedure was new and the outcomes were heavily influenced by the proficiency and degree of synergy of the team performing it. The error rate was quoted at about 4 percent, and Dr. N. later said that in 300 surgeries his team had established an error rate of 2.5 percent. I took an older friend—who had been a mentor to me and many of my friends—to lunch and ran through the logic with him: I had to trade a potential 2.5 percent greater chance of missing lymph node involvement for the avoidance of what I felt was almost certain permanent loss of function. I chose SLNB.

Surgery Day

The day of surgery came so quickly; it was dizzying. Talking about it gives me the opportunity to tell about my wife and how she supported me through this whole journey. Her name is Elizabeth, but she is called Happy, and she really deserves to have been mentioned earlier because she is so strong and has so much common sense, medical and otherwise. She even subscribes to two medical journals! We arrived at the hospital so early it was still dark, and she was with me during the first part of the procedure in Nuclear Medicine. This involved the injection of a radioactive tracer at the tumor site, which was tracked on a detector screen to find the "sentinel" lymph node. . . .

The next thing I remember was that I was on my way home, with Happy driving, in the dark of the evening. With the pain meds I really felt pretty good, and I was very thankful that I didn't have to stay in the hospital. The most salient feature of my chest at that time was a large bandage covering a drainage tube with a reservoir attached to the end of it. We had been taught a fairly complex procedure, which included measuring the amount of drainage and keeping track of it, and then disposing of it without triggering an infection. I remember a definite instruction not to wash out the reservoir, or, it said in very large type, I would have a "VERY BIG INFECTION." That was enough to convince both of us to be extremely careful, and Happy did a superb job caring for the drainage apparatus!

The next few days were somewhat of a blur, but pretty soon I was back in Dr. N.'s office with Happy receiving the news that one of the lymph nodes did have some cancer involvement. The magic number was 3, however, and I had less than three nodes involved. In that sense the news was good, but the doctors definitely wanted me to have chemotherapy. . . .

I learned that men get breast cancer about one one-hundredth as often as women, and in general are not offered nearly enough education about it. But my road would follow the same path as a woman's, with all the same fears and struggles. A man does have the benefit of two exceptions to this equality: I did not feel that my body image was threatened in the same way as a woman's by the loss of a breast, and my loss of hair, which was never complete, was an annoyance but not a source of any great embarrassment. . . .

Chemotherapy News

This was also the point in my journey when I received the news about what I should do for chemotherapy. My oncologist sent me for a number of tests, among which was something called a MUGA, which stands for some fancy words that relate to the ability of your heart to tolerate the rigors of chemotherapy. He said that mine was not bad but not on the strong side. That statement made me feel somewhat inadequate, because it seemed to mean that I was not able to undertake the very strongest treatment. But he recommended a somewhat "milder" cocktail given over nine treatments instead of the stronger mixture for four treatments. He reassured me that it was the "gold standard," and would have an equal beneficial effect. But it did mean that I would be on chemotherapy for about 7 months. And he was anxious to start right away.

A small extra bit of surgery that people should know about was the insertion of a MediPort. This is a device under the skin of either the chest or the arm—mine was in my chest on the side opposite the mastectomy—which allows the chemotherapy to be administered without always having to find a peripheral vein in which to insert the IV. Especially for people having the stronger forms of chemotherapy this is a very desirable strategy because the chemicals can be irritating to the veins. For me it made it much easier to have chemo and much less painful. . . .

The "Ice Trick"

One of the drugs in my chemo mix was notorious for causing sores in the mouth, and I was taught a technique of holding ice water in my mouth when that drug was administered. It is called hydrotherapy, and the rule was you had to keep ice water in your mouth for 45 minutes. This was just to keep the blood vessels in my mouth constricted, not for the purpose of swallowing any of the water. What I am talking about here should not be confused with hydration, which is a necessary routine to keep the body supplied with water by drinking at least eight glasses a day. I was instructed that hydration is important for carrying away the products of the chemo, and works very well.

I don't know why but I really disliked the ice water trick. I got to the point that doing it during chemo actually nauseated me. Even the sound of ice clinking in a glass caused a negative reaction, and just writing this I can feel the revulsion for the ice water over that period of time. It was a small thing but they kept insisting on 45 minutes, but that last 15 minutes was just hell. Between chemo sessions I dived into the Internet and found a clinical study in which patients had used hydrotherapy for 30 minutes and 45 minutes, and 30 minutes worked just as well. I marched in with a printout of the study and announced that I was only going to gag for 30 minutes and not 45. My chemo nurse said, "Mr. Rands, why do I not put it past you to find a clinical trial to prove your point?" From then on it was 30 minutes. . . .

Balancing Decisions

The balance between going along with professional advice and making my own decisions became more serious when I started using Neupogen. This is truly a wonder drug, but very expensive, which was luckily not an issue due to our excellent health insurance. Chemotherapy kills cancer cells, but it also kills a portion of the white cells in your blood, which are the infection fighters. My normal white cell count of around 3,000 went down to 1,000 or so 5 to 7 days after chemotherapy, low enough that I was relatively helpless against all the normal bugs that float around. I had to postpone one of my chemo sessions because my counts were too low, so I, like so many people before me, really needed help to recover from the depressing effects on my blood chemistry. Neupogen is a miraculous biotechnology drug that "gooses" up the white count, and this drug really works! It comes in small vials and is administered once a day under the skin with a hypodermic needle, for a period of days following the chemo infusion. The oncology office routinely told me to take ten shots. When I came in for a blood test my white count would be 30,000+, so I began refusing to take ten shots. After each chemo I took five and it worked just fine, with my count up to 5,000 or 6,000. I had to fight a bit for that piece of autonomy, but I finally prevailed. . . .

One challenge that shook me greatly was caused by a friendly gesture from a close associate. He had some contacts at another cancer institute nearby, and wanted me to get a second opinion about my chemotherapy. I actually talked to one of the doctors, who said my chemo regime was all wrong and I should have a much higher "dose intensity." He actually gave me some copies of scholarly papers on the subject, and I read them carefully. In the end, I decided to stick with the people I trusted.

The HER2 Issue

This is about a cellular growth gene called HER2/neu that, when it is overexpressed, indicates that the cancer is very aggressive and needs to be dealt with differently. As a consequence of my 2+ evaluation the oncologist recommended four more treatments with a different drug, so I actually had thirteen chemo treatments. Those last four treatments were really tough. I was told that some people had an immediate severe reaction to the drug, which would happen during the first few minutes of the first infusion. I really was scared. We waited anxiously, but fortunately it did not happen. I usually stayed home in bed for a day with achy flu-like symptoms after each treatment. It also made my hair fall out faster, and with each infusion my fingernails and toenails stopped growing for a day. After four treatments there were four little transverse creases in each fingernail and toenail at intervals of a half-millimeter or so, which I took to be the equivalent of the 3-week interval between treatments. In about 4 months they grew out to the ends of my nails and were gone. . . .

Another consequence of the report from the HER/2 test was that the usual follow-up treatment with Tamoxifen was not recommended because of the "positive" HER2. But in fact the test that I had for HER2 turned out to be obsolescent and in the process of being replaced by something called a FISH test. After my chemo was completed I requested a FISH test and it came back negative for HER2 overexpression! At first the mix-up bothered me, but about that time my oncologist retired and the oncologist that succeeded him on my case reassured me that I was much better off because of the extra chemo treatments. He also recommended another drug called Arimidex instead of Tamoxifen because follow-up treatment has been shown to be very beneficial.

The Radiation Question

All during my chemotherapy, which because of the extra four treatments took the better part of a year, I was concerned about whether I was going to get a recommendation for a course of radiation. I did not want it, but I did not feel that this was something I could refuse if it came along. I did, however, do as much research as I could. What I found was that in general I would not be a candidate for radiation because I had had a modified radical mastectomy, meaning that the delicate question of margins around the tumor had been removed.

There was one qualification to that good news, however. If the tumor were of a type that "crumbles" and leaves the area around it and any involved lymph nodes strewn with dangerous crumbs of tumor, radiation would be appropriate. I went into my appointment with the radiation oncologist thinking that I was going to say something very wise and philosophical, like, "Well, I am happy not to have radiation but that's good and bad news, because you are saying to me that this isn't a tool that will reduce my chances of a recurrence." Harrumph harrumph. When the time came to hear the words and she said that she was not going to recommend radiation, I was so happy that all I did was burst into tears!

Now a Survivor

It was in the late fall of 2000, just about a year after I found that lump in the shower, when my journey of being a patient gave way, in my mind at least, to a journey of survivorship. I was still on a pretty short leash, with checkups every 6 months and then finally every year. At first each checkup was a threat. What if the cancer came back? I had blood tests and mammograms, and I asked about repeating the bone scan but was told I did not need it. Gradually I became more comfortable with the checkups, and I am thankful that they have become less frequent.

I was living life again and loving it. However, if I ever get caught saying that life went back to "normal," I would not want that to be interpreted as meaning that it is just like it was before the cancer. I view life as being much more fragile and valuable than I did before. During my journey I lost three close friends to cancer, one of whom was my doctor, and another very close friend to a burst aorta. This has all made me that much more thankful for my survival and that of those who are still with me. . . .

The Cancer Survivor Role

There is a role that I think cancer survivors have an obligation to play. I call it a "pastoral" role. It has to do with spreading education about cancer and helping people not to feel so helpless. I have said to every group of people whom I have had the opportunity to address, and especially to men, that when you are in the shower and you are all soapy and your skin is slippery, just keep your mind a bit alert. If you feel anything you don't think should be there, have it checked out. Do not ignore it because you are a man and you don't think you can get breast cancer. I have been on TV and radio, taken part in cancer walks, and raised money for research. But the most important thing to do is to urge people to fight back and not feel so intimidated.

I feel in this regard that I have a new power, when I talk with someone who has just been diagnosed or is going through treatment, I don't have that old awkward feeling like cancer is this big black mystery that we can't really talk about. I used to say, "Wow, we're pulling for you," or something equally inane. That was, of course, always a sincere statement, but now when I talk with a cancer patient we are friends instantly, members of a club that is full of warmth and mutual support. We would not have chosen to join this club, but it nevertheless gives us a bond with each other that I would never have understood had I not experienced it. I immediately say, "How is your treatment going?" and "What are you taking?" and "Have you thought about doing this or that to make it easier?" And we do a lot of hugging and cheering for each other. We can't change each other's journey, which for some of us will lead back to normal life and for some of us will not, but we are on it together and we go along hand in hand, with the help of family and friends, and doctors and nurses who have new tools every day to help us.

Pregnancy and Breast Cancer

Andrea Gurwitt

Andrea Gurwitt is a New Jersey–based features writer. In the following article she tells the story of Regina Stuve, a publicist for Universal Music Group Nashville. Gurwitt describes Stuve's experience of finding a lump in her breast while pregnant with her first child. Instead of having chemotherapy while pregnant, Stuve chose to have labor induced immediately, although she was not due to give birth for another six weeks. In addition to having a newborn baby, Stuve also endured the emotional difficulties of losing her hair to chemotherapy and the exhaustion of undergoing chemotherapy and radiation treatments. The love and support of friends and family were as vital as the medical treatment she received.

Nathaniel saved her life.

That's what Regina Stuve believes and what her doctor says is entirely possible.

Regina was seven months pregnant with Nate when she found a lump in her left breast while putting on

SOURCE: Andrea Gurwitt, "Life, Interrupted," *Ladies' Home Journal,* October 2007, pp. 178, 180. Copyright © 2007 Meredith Corporation. All rights reserved. Reproduced by permission.

sunscreen. She was going for the last boat ride of the summer, her Fendi sunglasses and a straw cowboy hat firmly in place. It was September 4, 2006, Labor Day.

"Don't worry," people said. "You're pregnant; your breasts get lumpy."

Up till then she'd had the kind of life where everything did turn out to be fine. She was a 36-year-old publicist for Universal Music Group Nashville, in Tennessee, married for seven years to Ron Stuve, 45, vice president of artists and repertoire at BMG Music Publishing. They had a chocolate Labrador, Lucy, and lived in a 1940s stone Tudor house 10 minutes from her job. Regina worked with country music stars like Reba McEntire, Vince Gill and Josh Turner. She had a personal trainer, ate well and had never been seriously sick.

Biopsy Leads to Cancer Diagnosis

An ultrasound on September 27 showed something. You have an 80 percent chance it's nothing, her doctor told her, but he did a biopsy that same day, just to be sure.

On October 2, Regina got the call at work. She had breast cancer. Her world stopped. Although some researchers believe some treatments can be safe, she resisted the idea of having chemotherapy while she was still pregnant. "I literally put my fingers in my ears, saying 'lalala,' when the doctor tried to talk to me about it," she said.

An Early Birth

The next day her gynecologist told her Nate was big enough for her to have induced labor. The following morning, now 34 weeks into the pregnancy, Nate was born, at five pounds, 12 ounces.

Nine days later, with Nate still in the hospital for monitoring, doctors removed Regina's breast and with it an aggressive (stage-2) cancer that had not yet spread to the lymph nodes. Because it was hormone positive, her pregnancy hormones may indeed have made it show up faster.

Treatment Starts Right Away

The surgery was followed by five months of exhausting chemotherapy and six weeks of daily radiation. All that, plus a newborn, meant Regina needed help with everything. Her mother, Brenda Stephens, moved in for a time to tend to Regina. When Regina didn't have enough energy to wash her face, her mom washed it for her and rubbed cream into her dry skin. Ron calls Brenda "the most valuable player in all this." Meanwhile, Ron tended to Nate.

The country music world circled the family. Stars and execs celebrated Nate's birth, brought in food during the long recovery, and sent flowers, gifts and many e-mails

A surgeon finishes a mastectomy on a female patient. After surgery the patient could go through months of chemotherapy. (DY Riess MD/Alamy)

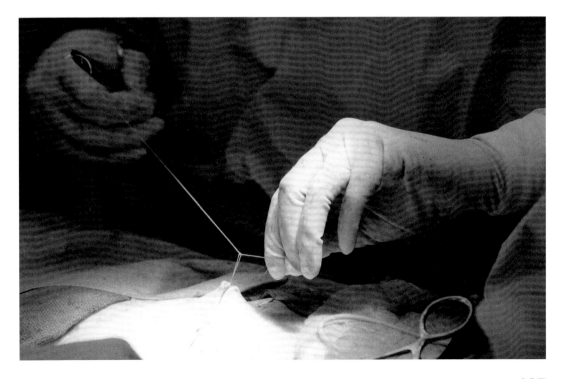

of concern—including one sent by Reba McEntire, who also paid for Regina's two wigs and gave her a personalized quilt for Nate's nursery.

"The warm embrace that I feel from my friends in the music industry continues to lift my spirit and gives me strength," Regina wrote in her journal in November.

Hair Loss Is Difficult

The part that hit her hardest emotionally was losing her long blond hair. It was even harder than not breastfeeding, since she could hold Nate close to bottle-feed him. Once, outside a market in Florida where the family vacationed . . . after her last radiation treatment, a little boy looked up at the person in the big straw hat, sunglasses and long-sleeved shirt and said, "Is that a lady, Mommy?" Regina is not a crier, but she cried about this. A hair/makeup artist friend made hair extensions on strips that Regina could Velcro into her hats.

Regina's hair has grown to half an inch now. She and Ron joke that the whole family has the same hairstyle, Nate included. Because her cancer was both hormone and HER2 positive, she'll take Herceptin (for HER2) until February 2008 and Tamoxifen (to deal with hormones) for five years. The combination of the two drugs is designed to help lower the risk of recurrence, according to her oncologist, David Johnson, M.D., director of the division of hematology/oncology at the Vanderbilt-Ingram Cancer Center. She plans to have breast-reconstruction surgery after Christmas [2006].

One Year Later

Regina went back to work in July [2007]. Her boss sent her flowers, and her coworkers told her she didn't look sick at all.

And on October 4, the boy who saved his mother's life turns a year old.

Implants and Breast Cancer

Jenn Lyon as told to Cynthia Wang

In the following article Cynthia Wang presents an interview with Jenn Lyon, a contestant on *Survivor: Palau* in 2004. When Lyon found a lump in her breast she assumed it was scar tissue due to the breast implants she had gotten six years previously. After a year she found another lump, which turned out to be cancer. Lyon describes how she had reconstructive surgery before starting her chemotherapy treatments and how that surgery gave her an enormous emotional boost. She also talks about the ramifications of having chemotherapy and other drug treatments on her future plans to have children.

I t seemed like it came on quickly. In the summer of 2004, I felt something in my right breast that didn't feel normal. They always describe cancer in terms of a pea, right? Well, this was more like several rocks strung together. I thought it was probably scar tissue related to my breast implants. So I let it go—for a long time.

SOURCE: As told to Cynthia Wang by Jenn Lyon, "Rebuilding a Body, Restoring a Soul," *People*, vol. 64, October 24, 2005, pp. 103–104. Copyright © 2005 Time, Inc. Reproduced by permission.

FAST FACT

About 20 percent of all breast implants in the United States are used for breast reconstruction due to cancer.

I got my saline implants six years ago [in 1999]. It was just something in my head that I thought I needed to do for self-esteem, to balance myself out. Before, I was a large A-cup, and the implants changed me to a small C-cup. I always thought I was kind of a flat-chest, round-butt kind of person. I didn't think my parents would have understood. Can you imagine lying to your mom about not having bigger boobs? I was like, "Oh, it must be the shirt."

At the time I noticed the lumps I didn't have insurance, which was a big part of why I didn't get it checked immediately. I went on the Internet and thought, "It is scar tissue. No big deal." But a year later, I felt another lump right in the center of the breast and something in my right armpit. I saw a surgeon who said, "I'm pretty sure you have breast cancer." After a mammogram, an ultrasound and a biopsy, it was confirmed—stage III.

I've been healthy my whole life. I didn't feel bad the day I was diagnosed with breast cancer, and I don't feel bad today. It's strange to know you can be walking around, feeling fine, and have something like this inside you. Fortunately, my sister Kim goes with me to everything; she helped me go over my options. One doctor wanted to do chemotherapy to shrink the tumors. Another was adamant that I have surgery right away because, if I did chemo first, there was a chance the tumors could stay or even metastasize. I opted for a modified, radical bilateral mastectomy on Aug. 29 [2005] at Cedars-Sinai Medical Center in Los Angeles. A surgeon removed both my breasts and 29 lymph nodes. Sometimes, I just let myself be upset about it. I don't hold back, and it's usually when I'm by myself. If you can take that time to kind of grieve, I think it helps a lot. If I didn't do this, I think it would eat me up.

It took a good three weeks to really look in the mirror. The first thing that came into my head is, "What has happened? I'm butchered!" I had already decided to have reconstruction. After my mastectomy, a plastic surgeon put in "spacers" to expand my chest muscles to make room for the new implants—smaller silicone implants this time. A second operation Oct. 5 completed the process.

My new implants have been a huge boost to my spirit. It's still summer here in California, you know, and I'm in a short-sleeved shirt and I can't imagine what it would be like completely without anything underneath it. Right now, I am about the size I was before the original implants. And it feels good.

Many women prefer to have breast implant surgery after a mastectomy. **(Medical-on-Line/Alamy)**

In a week or so, I start a four- to six-month course of chemotherapy, followed by tamoxifen, a drug designed to prevent a recurrence. My doctor has warned me I may stop having my period and go into early menopause. That's tough because I haven't had kids yet. I've always thought about adopting, and my boyfriend, Brian Smith [who competed on *The Amazing Race* with his brother Greg], and I both have adopted siblings. But seriously, five months after we've been dating, to have to ask him if he will consider fertility treatment? He said it's something we can work through. Brian is only 28 and I've had to put some big stuff on him. He has not faltered. I'm very lucky.

Being on *Survivor* has helped in every sense of the word. My doctor told me, "You have beautiful hair, and you're going to lose it." But Coby Archa, the Texas hairdresser who was in my *Survivor* tribe, says he's going to shave my head for me—and shave his too. *Survivor* taught me there's an end in sight. As hard as it is, it will be over, and you have to appreciate every day.

GLOSSARY

adjuvant therapy   Treatment given after the primary treatment (usually surgery) to increase the chance of being cured. Adjuvant therapy may include radiation, chemotherapy, hormone therapy, or biological therapy.

aspiration   The removal of fluid from a lump or cyst using a needle.

benign tumor   A noncancerous growth of tissue.

biopsy   The removal of tissues or cells for examination by a pathologist to check for disease or damage.

carcinoma   Cancer that starts in the lining of an organ.

cell   An individual unit of protoplasm. Every animal and plant is made up of one or more cells.

chemotherapy   Cancer treatment using anticancer drugs. This type of treatment may be given before or after surgery. Systemic chemotherapy uses the bloodstream to dispense the drugs throughout the body. Regional chemotherapy places the drugs directly into a body cavity, an organ, or the spinal column.

chest wall   The muscles, bones, and joints that make up the area of the body between the neck and the abdomen.

clinical trial   A research program using real patients that evaluates a certain type of treatment, drug, or procedure. Clinical trials often lead to widespread use of improved methods of treatment. These studies can also be referred to as clinical studies.

core biopsy   A needle biopsy procedure using a large-gauge needle.

ductal carcinoma in situ   Cancer that stays inside the milk duct without invading the surrounding breast tissue.

ducts	Tubes in the breast that transport milk to the nipple during breast-feeding.
early stage breast cancer	Cancer that is usually confined to the ducts or lobes and is known as noninvasive.
estrogen	A female hormone that can be either natural or synthetic.
excisional biopsy	An entire lump or area of suspicion that is removed for testing.
hormone therapy	Cancer treatment that stops cancer cells from growing by removing hormones or obstructing the action of hormones.
implant	A fluid-filled sac, usually silicone or saline, surgically implanted above or below the chest muscles to restore breast shape after breast cancer surgery.
incisional biopsy	A biopsy in which only a small sample of tissue is removed for testing.
invasive stage breast cancer	Cancer that spreads beyond the ducts or lobes into the surrounding breast tissue.
lobes	Areas of the breast that contain the smaller lobules. There are fifteen to twenty lobes within each breast.
lobular carcinoma in situ	Cancer that stays in the lobules without invading the surrounding breast tissue.
lobules	Small areas of the breast that produce milk. These are located within the larger lobe area of the breast.
lumpectomy	Removal of breast cancer along with a small amount of the normal surrounding tissue. The surgery may include removal of lymph nodes in the underarms.
lymphatic fluid	Fluid that moves through the body's lymphatic system and carries cells that fight infection and disease.
lymph node	A mass of lymphatic tissue that filters lymphatic fluid and stores white blood cells. They may also be referred to as lymph glands.

lymphoedema	An abnormal collection of lymphatic fluid in the body's tissues.
malignant	Cancerous growth of tissue.
mammogram	An X-ray of the breast.
mastectomy	Surgical removal of breast tissue. There are several different levels of mastectomy depending on the stage of the cancer, including partial, total, modified radical, and radical.
metastasize	Spread from one area or region of the body to another.
metastatic stage breast cancer	Breast cancer that has spread to other areas of the body.
modified radical mastectomy	Surgical removal of the entire breast along with the lining above the chest muscles, some of the lymph nodes in the underarm area, and in some cases, part of the chest wall muscles.
needle biopsy	A fluid or tissue sample removed with a needle.
oncologist	A physician that specializes in the treatment of cancer.
partial mastectomy	Surgical removal of the area of the breast that has cancer in it, along with a small amount of normal surrounding tissue. The surgery may include removal of lymph nodes in the underarms. This procedure can also be referred to as a segmental mastectomy.
progesterone	A hormone that has a part in pregnancy and the menstrual cycle.
prognosis	The outlook for recovery from a disease.
radiation therapy	Cancer treatment that uses X-rays or other kinds of radiation to kill or stall the growth of cancer cells. There are two types of this treatment: external, using a machine to bombard the cancer from outside the body; and internal, using a radioactive substance (usually seeds, wires, or catheters) to dispense radiation from inside the body.

radical mastectomy	Surgery to remove the entire breast along with all underarm lymph nodes and all chest wall muscles.
remission	The decrease or disappearance of the symptoms of a disease.
sentinel lymph node	The first lymph node in the underarm area to receive lymphatic drainage from a tumor.
sentinel lymph node biopsy	The removal of the sentinel lymph node for examination.
systemic therapy	Cancer treatment that reaches all cells of the body.
tamoxifen	A drug used to treat breast cancer. Some of the more severe side effects are liver damage, blood clots, and an increased risk of endometrial cancer.
total mastectomy	Surgery to remove the entire breast that has cancer; may include removing lymph nodes in the underarms. This procedure may also be referred to as a simple mastectomy.
tumor	An abnormal growth of tissue. A tumor can be malignant or benign.

CHRONOLOGY

B.C.

ca. 500–3000 The earliest descriptions of breast cancer, found in an Egyptian papyrus.

A.D.

ca. 100–200 Breast cancer is claimed to be caused by an excess of black bile.

ca. 400–500 Hippocrates describes hard tumors in the breast area.

ca. 500–600 The court physician for Byzantine empress Theodora recommends breast removal for her cancerlike illness.

1811 Nabby Adams, daughter of John and Abigail Adams, undergoes mastectomy surgery for her advanced breast cancer.

1882 Radical mastectomy is developed by surgeon William Halsted.

1895 The first surgical techniques for reconstructive surgery following mastectomy are used. The first X-ray treatment for cancer is given.

1905 Staging of breast cancer is first used. It will not become widely used in many countries until the 1950s.

1913 German surgeon Albert Salomon discovers different types of breast cancer.

1927 British surgeon Geoffrey Keynes ceases using radical mastectomy and begins using a more conservative approach to breast cancer surgery.

1936 The Women's Field Army is founded in the United States to help make the public aware of the fight against breast cancer.

1940 The Manchester Classification System for staging breast cancer is developed by Ralston Paterson.

1943 The TNM Classification System is developed by Pierre Denois. The Columbia Clinical Classification System is developed by Cushman Haagensen and Arthur Stout.

1946 Injections of muscatine (a compound related to the chemical warfare agent nitrogen mustard) are found to reduce tumor size in a patient with lymphoma.

1947 Breast cancer is reported to be the leading cause of death from cancer for women in the United States. It is also reported to be the most common form of cancer for women.

1948 The modified radical mastectomy is developed.

1950 The first breast cancer public education film, *Breast Self-Examination*, is released by the American Cancer Society and the National Cancer Institute.

1957 Charles Heidelberger discovers 5-fluorouracil. This chemotherapy agent is still used to treat breast cancer.

1962 Tamoxifen is discovered.

1963   Silicone is first used for breast reconstruction.

1965   Combination chemotherapy is first used. This treatment strategy is still in use today.

1967   Paclitaxel is discovered. It will become a major part of later breast cancer treatments.

1972   Adjuvant chemotherapy is used on a trial basis.

1974   First Lady Betty Ford is diagnosed with breast cancer and speaks about it openly.

1978   Tamoxifen is approved by the FDA to treat estrogen-receptor-positive breast cancer.

1983   The National Cancer Institute sponsors phase one clinical trials of the cancer drug paclitaxel.

1985   Lumpectomy plus radiation therapy is shown to be equivalent to mastectomy for survival of breast cancer.

1990s   Many breast cancer advocacy groups are formed during this decade.

1990   Breast cancer gene BRCA1 is found on a specific site on chromosome 17.

1998   Herceptin (trastuzumab) is shown to improve survival rates for women with advanced stages of breast cancer.

1999   Physician Jerri Nielson is evacuated from the South Pole after discovering a lump in her breast and performing her own biopsies and initial chemotherapy treatments.

1999   Trastuzumab is approved for use in patients with HER2-positive breast cancer.

2001   *The New England Journal of Medicine* reports that patients with HER2-positive breast cancer who are treated with trastuzumab have improved survival rates compared to those treated with chemotherapy alone.

2002   The World Health Organization reports that breast cancer mortality is reduced by 35 percent in women aged fifty to sixty-nine who are screened for the disease.

2003   Breast cancer stem cells are discovered by researchers at the Michigan Comprehensive Cancer Center.

2005   Herceptin plus chemotherapy given after surgery is shown to reduce the risk of breast cancer recurrence.

2006   Eating more than one and a half servings of red meat per day is shown to increase the risk of hormone-receptor-positive breast cancer.

2007   The death rate from breast cancer in the United States continues to drop at the rate of roughly 2 percent per year.

2008   A screening test for breast cancer is being developed using an individual's saliva to detect the presence of cancer.

ORGANIZATIONS TO CONTACT

African American Breast Cancer Alliance, Inc.
PO Box 8981
Minneapolis, MN 55408
(612) 825-3675
fax: (612) 827-2977
www.aabcainc.org

This organization provides education, awareness, and support for breast cancer patients, their families, and the community, focusing on African Americans and people of color. The Web site provides links to various other breast cancer information sites.

American Cancer Society
15999 Clifton Rd. NE
Atlanta, GA 30329
(800) 227-2345
www.cancer.org

The American Cancer Society is a nationwide, community-based health organization with over thirty-four hundred local offices. The society's goal is to eliminate cancer as a health issue and to help fight cancer through research, education, patient service, advocacy, and rehabilitation.

American Institute for Cancer Research
1759 R St. NW
Washington, DC 20009
(202) 328-7744
(800) 843-8114
www.aicr.org

This organization concentrates on providing information on cancer prevention, mainly through diet, weight management, and physical activity. It also offers cancer pamphlets for the general public and a cancer resource guide for patients and their families.

National Cancer Institute
6116 Executive Blvd., Rm. 3036A
Bethesda, MD 20892-8322
(800) 422-6237
www.cancer.gov

This government institute, part of the National Institutes of Health, is the principal government agency for cancer research and training. The institute provides detailed information on all types of cancer and free information is provided upon request. A live helpline is also available through the Web site.

National Women's Health Information Center
8270 Willow Oaks Corporate Dr.
Fairfax, VA 22031
(800) 994-9662
www.4women.gov

This government program, part of the Office on Women's Health in the U.S. Department of Health and Human Services, specifically addresses women's health issues through developing health programs, educating health professionals, and disseminating women's health information to the general public. The center has information on more than eight hundred health topics and offers health publications, statistics, daily news, and calendars of health events.

Susan G. Komen for the Cure
5005 LBJ Fwy.,
Ste. 250
Dallas, TX 75244
(877) 465-6636
http://cms.komen.org

Formerly known as the Susan G. Komen Breast Cancer Foundation, this grassroots network focuses on breast cancer education and research. Since its inception in 1982, the foundation has spent nearly $1 billion on research, education, and health services. Many local chapters are available for community-based aid, and a breast care helpline is available nationally.

Y-ME National Breast Cancer Organization
212 W. Van Buren,
Ste. 1000
Chicago, IL
60607-3913
(312) 986-8338
(800) 221-2141
fax: (312) 294-8597
www.y-me.org

Y-ME is an information, services, and support organization for breast cancer patients. It offers a twenty-four-hour hotline staffed by breast cancer survivors, in addition to many informational booklets and brochures about different breast cancer issues.

Young Survival Coalition
61 Broadway,
Ste. 2235
New York, NY 10006
(646) 257-3000
(877) 972-1011
fax: (646) 257-3030
www.youngsurvival
.org

This nonprofit organization specifically addresses issues and concerns connected with young women and breast cancer. The coalition operates through action, advocacy, and awareness to educate the medical community and the general population about the special issues that young breast cancer patients face.

FOR FURTHER READING

Books

American Cancer Society, *American Cancer Society Complete Guide to Breast Cancer.* Atlanta: American Cancer Society, 2008.

David Chan, *Breast Cancer: Real Questions, Real Answers.* New York: Marlowe, 2006.

Edward J. Conley, *The Breast Cancer Prevention Plan.* New York: McGraw-Hill, 2006.

Deanna Favre, *Don't Bet Against Me! Beating the Odds Against Breast Cancer and in Life.* Carol Stream, IL: Tyndale House, 2007.

Maureen Keene, *What to Eat If You Have Cancer.* New York: McGraw-Hill, 2006.

Debbie Leifert, Gina Castronovo, Tamara Brennan, Jackie Ehrlich, Cindy Goldberg, and Donna Palmisciano, *Just a Lump in the Road . . . : Reflections of Young Breast Cancer Survivors.* Lincoln, NE: iUniverse, 2007.

Kenneth D. Miller, ed., *Choices in Breast Cancer Treatment: Medical Specialists and Cancer Survivors Tell You What You Need to Know.* Baltimore: Johns Hopkins University Press, 2008.

James S. Olson, *Bathsheba's Breast: Women, Cancer, and History.* Baltimore: Johns Hopkins University Press, 2005.

Lillie Shockney, *Navigating Breast Cancer: A Guide for the Newly Diagnosed.* Sudbury, MA: Jones and Bartlett, 2007.

———, *Stealing Second Base: A Breast Cancer Survivor's Experience and Breast Cancer Expert's Story.* Sudbury, MA: Jones and Bartlett, 2007.

Terry L. Smith, *Breast Cancer: Current and Emerging Trends in Detection and Treatment.* New York: Rosen, 2006.

Jack Willis, *Saving Jack: A Man's Struggle with Breast Cancer.* Norman: University of Oklahoma Press, 2008.

Periodicals

Amy Cohen, "Fighting Chance," *Vogue*, October 2007.

Francesca Coltrera, "Breast Cancer: New Ways to Beat the Odds," *Good Housekeeping*, October 2007.

Mary A. Fischer, "The Breast Cancer Nobody Is Talking About," *Oprah Magazine*, October 2007.

Liz Galst, "Think Pink, Healthy You: Breast Health," *Better Homes and Gardens*, October 2007.

Sharony Green, "We Beat Breast Cancer," *Essence*, October 2007.

Bernadine Healy, "The Heart After Breast Cancer," *U.S. News & World Report*, October 29, 2007.

Katherine Hobson, "Density Danger," *U.S. News & World Report*, February 12, 2007.

———, "To Screen—or Not?" *U.S. News & World Report*, April 23, 2007.

Beth Howard, "Winning the War on Cancer," *Prevention*, November 2007.

Kathleen Kingsbury, "The Changing Face of Breast Cancer," *Time*, October 15, 2007.

Susan Love and Sue Rochman, "Sharper Focus? Women Should Demand More Inventive Breast Cancer Research—Not Just More MRIs," *Ms.*, Fall 2007.

Tedd Mitchell, "The Latest Cancer Breakthroughs," *USA Weekend*, September 28–30, 2007.

Alice Park, "Breast Cancer Basics," *Time*, October 15, 2007.

Tara Parker-Pope, "The Cancer Connection," *Ladies Home Journal*, March 2007.

Patrick Perry, "Targeting Breast Cancer," *Saturday Evening Post*, November/December 2007.

Roni Caryn Rabin, "Study Finds Rise in Choice of Double Mastectomies," *New York Times*, October 23, 2007.

Hallie Levine Sklar, "Who Gets Breast Cancer and Who Survives?" *Redbook*, October 2007.

Claudia Wallis and Alice Park, "Living with Cancer," *Time*, April 9, 2007.

Rick Weiss, "Lights at Night Are Linked to Breast Cancer," *Washington Post*, February 20, 2008.

Patricia Wendling, "Cancer Detection Enhanced, but at a Price," *Family Practice News*, December 15, 2007.

Internet Sources

American Cancer Society, "Can Having an Abortion Cause or Contribute to Breast Cancer?" August 6, 2007. www.cancer.org.

CNN, "Genetic Testing for Breast Cancer: Who's It For?" November 20, 2006. www.cnn.com/HEALTH/library/HQ/ 00350 .html.

Amy Harmon, "Cancer Free at 33, but Weighing a Mastectomy," *New York Times*, September 16, 2007. www.nytimes.com.

University of Chicago Medical Center, "Personalized Medicine Can Cut Breast Cancer Risk," *ScienceDaily*, February 19, 2008. www.sciencedaily.com.

INDEX